Getting Started with PowerShell

Learn the fundamentals of PowerShell to build reusable scripts and functions to automate administrative tasks with Windows

Michael Shepard

[PACKT] open source*

PUBLISHING

community experience distilled

BIRMINGHAM - MUMBAI

Getting Started with PowerShell

First published: August 2015

Production reference: 1210815

Published by Packt Publishing Ltd.
Livery Place
35 Livery Street
Birmingham B3 2PB, UK.

ISBN 978-1-78355-850-6

www.packtpub.com

Credits

Author

Michael Shepard

Reviewers

Richard Gibson

David Green

Keith Lindsay

Mayur Arvind Makwana

Ashley Poole

Acquisition Editors

Indrajit Das

Usha Iyer

Content Development Editor

Arwa Manasawala

Technical Editor

Ryan Kochery

Copy Editor

Kausambhi Majumdar

Project Coordinator

Shweta H Birwatkar

Proofreader

Safis Editing

Indexer

Tejal Daruwale Soni

Production Coordinator

Melwyn Dsa

Cover Work

Melwyn Dsa

About the Author

Michael Shepard has been working with computers since the early 1980s, starting with an Apple II at school and a Commodore 64 at home. He first worked in IT in 1989 and has been a full-time professional in this field since 1997. He has been working at Jack Henry and Associates since 2000. Mike's focus has changed over the years from being a database application developer to a DBA (an application administrator), and he is now a solutions architect. In his years as a DBA, he found PowerShell to be a critical component in creating the automation required to keep up with a growing set of servers and applications. He is active in the PowerShell community on StackOverflow and in the projects on CodePlex. He has been blogging about PowerShell since 2009 at https://powershellstation.com and is the author of *PowerShell Troubleshooting Guide* by Packt Publishing.

I'd like to thank my employer, Jack Henry and Associates, for allowing me the freedom to both learn and teach PowerShell over the last several years. My beautiful wife, Stephanie, and my children, Simeon and Gwen, continue to be a joy in my life, and the time when I'm not working on PowerShell is spent with them. Finally, I need to recognize the wonderfully supportive PowerShell community, which has encouraged me to learn and share PowerShell since its inception.

About the Reviewers

Richard Gibson lives in London and has worked as a .NET developer for 8 years. His work has brought him into the world of DevOps, and PowerShell has become a necessary skill for the automation of everyday tasks.

He is currently working for Asos.com (http://www.asos.com/) as a senior developer, spending most of his time with PowerShell to automate TeamCity to provide continuous deployment for the business. Richard blogs on various issues related to .NET and PowerShell at http://richiban.uk/.

David Green is an IT professional from the south of England with a wealth of experience in both the public and private sectors. Currently working for a leading food manufacturing company, he is always looking to provide robust and scalable solutions that contribute to business objectives.

Also, he writes a blog about his projects and the solutions he finds to the problems he encounters. He helps where he can and generally tries to learn something useful everyday. Contributing to this book has been another fortunate opportunity for David.

More information about him can be found on his website at http://www.tookitaway.co.uk.

> I'd like to thank my family, friends, and colleagues, who are always there for me whenever I need them and who have managed to make me the person that I am today. You should work, learn, play, and have fun. It's your intention, attitude, and what you do with your opportunities that sets you apart.

Keith Lindsay graduated from Sacred Heart University with honors and spent nearly a decade as a software engineer. After deciding to explore a new path, he moved to product management for Citrix ShareFile, where he uses his technical skills to help improve and promote APIs and SDKs. He is a big proponent of PowerShell and has helped his company develop a PowerShell SDK for file sharing. You can read more about using PowerShell for file sharing on his blog at `http://blogs.citrix.com/author/keithl1/`.

Mayur Arvind Makwana is a software professional with more than 5 years of experience in the field of IT. He has a degree in computer engineering. He is a huge believer in certifications, with his current certification acronyms including Microsoft, Citrix, and VMware technologies. His other certifications include:

- Citrix Certified Administrator for Citrix XenApp 6.5 (CCA)
- Microsoft Certified Professional (MCP)
- Microsoft Specialist [Microsoft Server Virtualization with Windows Server Hyper-V and System Center]
- VMware Certified Associate—Data Center Virtualization (VCA-DCV)
- ITIL (Information Technology Infrastructure Library) V3 Foundation
- ChangeBase AOK (Application Compatibility Testing and Remediation)
- OCA (Oracle Certified Associate)

Mayur has reviewed many technical books and written technical blogs. He has attended several courses and conducted training sessions on the following technologies:

- Licensing Windows Server
- Advanced Tools & Scripting with PowerShell 3.0 Jump Start
- Deploying Windows 8
- Licensing Windows 8
- Migrating from Windows XP to Windows 7
- Networking Fundamentals
- Introduction to Hyper-V Jump Start

Some other books Mayur has worked on include:

- Microsoft Application Virtualization Cookbook
- Windows PowerShell for .NET Developers
- TroubleShooting Citrix XenDesktop
- TroubleShooting Citrix XenApp

I would like to thank my mom, Beena Makwana, who has always encouraged me to utilize my potential and to share my expertise and knowledge with people. Thanks to the PACKT Publishing team for giving me this opportunity.

Ashley Poole is a highly motivated software support analyst with over 6 years of professional experience in the field of IT. Normally, he can be found exploring topics such as Microsoft SQL Server, C#, PowerShell, and DevOps.

Recently, he has been exploring software development technologies and practices as he has begun a journey into the world of software development.

Ashley can be found blogging on various IT and software topics on his website at www.ashleypoole.co.uk, tweeting at @AshleyPooleUK, or sharing open source projects and scripts for the community at https://github.com/AshleyPoole.

www.PacktPub.com

Support files, eBooks, discount offers, and more

For support files and downloads related to your book, please visit www.PacktPub.com.

Did you know that Packt offers eBook versions of every book published, with PDF and ePub files available? You can upgrade to the eBook version at www.PacktPub.com and as a print book customer, you are entitled to a discount on the eBook copy. Get in touch with us at service@packtpub.com for more details.

At www.PacktPub.com, you can also read a collection of free technical articles, sign up for a range of free newsletters and receive exclusive discounts and offers on Packt books and eBooks.

https://www2.packtpub.com/books/subscription/packtlib

Do you need instant solutions to your IT questions? PacktLib is Packt's online digital book library. Here, you can search, access, and read Packt's entire library of books.

Why subscribe?

- Fully searchable across every book published by Packt
- Copy and paste, print, and bookmark content
- On demand and accessible via a web browser

Free access for Packt account holders

If you have an account with Packt at www.PacktPub.com, you can use this to access PacktLib today and view 9 entirely free books. Simply use your login credentials for immediate access.

Table of Contents

Preface

Since its introduction in 2007, Windows PowerShell has become the *de facto* scripting solution for Windows system administrators and other IT professionals. With its extensive functionality and powerful language, PowerShell can be used to automate almost any area of the Windows ecosystem. If you haven't learned PowerShell yet, there's no time like the present. This book will guide you through the most important topics to begin your learning journey. If you have used PowerShell before but wish to have a refresher, this book should serve as a guide to the topics that you need to understand in order to be successful in using PowerShell for your scripting and automation needs.

What this book covers

Chapter 1, First Steps, covers the installation of Powershell and the validation of the installed version, as well as how to issue the first few commands.

Chapter 2, Building Blocks, introduces the "Big 3" cmdlets that reveal the workings of the PowerShell cmdlets.

Chapter 3, Objects and PowerShell, explains how the output in PowerShell is always an object, and how we can deal with these objects.

Chapter 4, Life on the Assembly Line, presents the PowerShell pipeline and the *-object cmdlets that provide a tremendous ability for data manipulation.

Chapter 5, Formatting Output, explains the PowerShell formatting system, including how the output is formatted by default, as well as how to control formatting.

Chapter 6, Scripts, shows how sequences of commands can be packaged into a reusable unit.

Chapter 7, Functions, explains how to use functions as a second way of building reusable blocks of code.

Chapter 8, Modules, demonstrates PowerShell's method of organizing code libraries.

Chapter 9, File I/O, shows several ways to work with files in PowerShell for input and output.

Chapter 10, WMI and CIM, explains how to access WMI repositories with the WMI and CIM cmdlets.

Chapter 11, Web Server Administration, demonstrates a few techniques to use PowerShell to administer the IIS web server.

Appendix, Next Steps, suggests some "next steps" that you will find useful as skills to add to your PowerShell repertoire.

What you need for this book

Most of the examples in the book will work with PowerShell Version 2.0 and above. In the sections where a higher version of the engine is required, it will be indicated in the text. You should have no problems running the provided code on either a client installation (Windows 7 or greater) or a server installation (Windows Server 2008 R2 or higher).

Who this book is for

This book is intended for the Windows administrators or DevOps users who need to use PowerShell to automate tasks. Whether you know nothing about PowerShell or know just enough to be dangerous, this guide will give you what you need to take your scripting ability to the next level.

Conventions

In this book, you will find a number of text styles that distinguish between different kinds of information. Here are some examples of these styles and an explanation of their meaning.

Code words in text, database table names, folder names, filenames, file extensions, pathnames, dummy URLs, user input, and Twitter handles are shown as follows: "Here we can see that the Get-ChildItem cmdlet has three aliases."

A block of code is set as follows:

```
ForEach ($placeholder in $collection){
  #Code goes here
}
```

Any command-line input or output is written as follows:

```
%WINDIR%\System32\WindowsPowerShell\v1.0\
```

New terms and **important words** are shown in bold. Words that you see on the screen, for example, in menus or dialog boxes, appear in the text like this: "On the shortcut tab of the properties window, press the **Advanced** button."

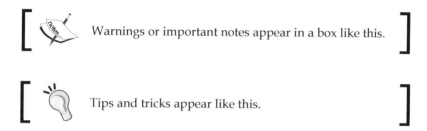

Warnings or important notes appear in a box like this.

Tips and tricks appear like this.

Reader feedback

Feedback from our readers is always welcome. Let us know what you think about this book—what you liked or disliked. Reader feedback is important for us as it helps us develop titles that you will really get the most out of.

To send us general feedback, simply e-mail feedback@packtpub.com, and mention the book's title in the subject of your message.

If there is a topic that you have expertise in and you are interested in either writing or contributing to a book, see our author guide at www.packtpub.com/authors.

Customer support

Now that you are the proud owner of a Packt book, we have a number of things to help you to get the most from your purchase.

Downloading the example code

You can download the example code files from your account at `http://www.packtpub.com` for all the Packt Publishing books you have purchased. If you purchased this book elsewhere, you can visit `http://www.packtpub.com/support` and register to have the files e-mailed directly to you.

Errata

Although we have taken every care to ensure the accuracy of our content, mistakes do happen. If you find a mistake in one of our books—maybe a mistake in the text or the code—we would be grateful if you could report this to us. By doing so, you can save other readers from frustration and help us improve subsequent versions of this book. If you find any errata, please report them by visiting `http://www.packtpub.com/submit-errata`, selecting your book, clicking on the **Errata Submission Form** link, and entering the details of your errata. Once your errata are verified, your submission will be accepted and the errata will be uploaded to our website or added to any list of existing errata under the Errata section of that title.

To view the previously submitted errata, go to `https://www.packtpub.com/books/content/support` and enter the name of the book in the search field. The required information will appear under the **Errata** section.

Piracy

Piracy of copyrighted material on the Internet is an ongoing problem across all media. At Packt, we take the protection of our copyright and licenses very seriously. If you come across any illegal copies of our works in any form on the Internet, please provide us with the location address or website name immediately so that we can pursue a remedy.

Please contact us at `copyright@packtpub.com` with a link to the suspected pirated material.

We appreciate your help in protecting our authors and our ability to bring you valuable content.

Questions

If you have a problem with any aspect of this book, you can contact us at `questions@packtpub.com`, and we will do our best to address the problem.

1
First Steps

In the world of Microsoft system administration, it is becoming impossible to avoid PowerShell. If you've never looked at PowerShell before or want a refresher to make sure you understand what is going on, this chapter would be a good place to start. We will cover the following topics:

- Determining the installed PowerShell version
- Installing/Upgrading PowerShell
- Starting a PowerShell session
- Simple PowerShell commands
- PowerShell Aliases

Determining the installed PowerShell version

There are many ways to determine which version of PowerShell, if any, is installed on a computer. We will examine how this information is stored in the registry and how to have PowerShell tell you the version.

 It's helpful while learning new things to actually follow along on the computer as much as possible. A big part of the learning process is developing "muscle memory", where you get used to typing the commands you see throughout the book. As you do this, it will also help you pay closer attention to the details in the code you see, since the code won't work correctly if you don't get the syntax right.

Using the registry to find the installed version

If you're running at least Windows 7 or Server 2008, you already have PowerShell installed on your machine. Windows XP and Server 2003 can install PowerShell, but it isn't pre-installed as part of the **Operating System (OS)**. To see if PowerShell is installed at all, no matter what OS is running, inspect the following registry entry:

```
HKLM\Software\Microsoft\PowerShell\1\Install
```

If this exists and contains the value of 1, PowerShell is installed. To see, using the registry, what version of PowerShell is installed, there are a couple of places to look at.

First, the following value will exist if PowerShell 3.0 or higher is installed:

```
HKLM\SOFTWARE\Microsoft\PowerShell\3\PowerShellEngine\PowerShellVersion
```

If this value exists, it will contain the PowerShell version that is installed. For instance, my Windows 7 computer is running PowerShell 4.0, so regedit.exe shows the value of 4.0 in that entry:

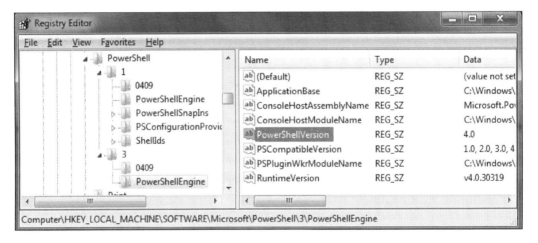

If this registry entry does not exist, you have either PowerShell 1.0 or 2.0 installed. To determine which, examine the following registry entry (note the 3 is changed to 1):

```
HKLM\SOFTWARE\Microsoft\PowerShell\1\PowerShellEngine\PowerShellVersion
```

This entry will either contain 1.0 or 2.0, to match the installed version of PowerShell.

It is important to note that all versions of PowerShell after 2.0 include the 2.0 engine, so this registry entry will exist for any version of PowerShell. For example, even if you have PowerShell 5.0 installed, you will also have the PowerShell 2.0 engine installed and will see both 5.0 and 2.0 in the registry.

Using PowerShell to find the installed version

No matter what version of PowerShell you have installed, it will be installed in the same place. This installation directory is called PSHOME and is located at:

```
%WINDIR%\System32\WindowsPowerShell\v1.0\
```

In this folder, there will be an executable file called PowerShell.exe. There should be a shortcut to this in your start menu, or in the start screen, depending on your operating system. In either of these, search for PowerShell and you should find it. Running this program opens the PowerShell console, which is present in all the versions.

At first glance, this looks like Command Prompt but the text (and perhaps the color) should give a clue that something is different:

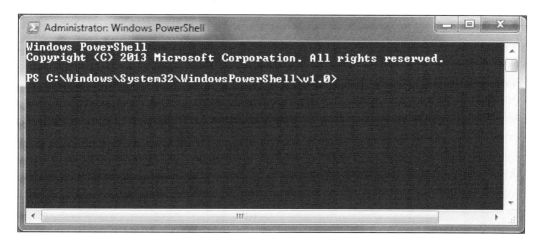

Downloading the example code

You can download the example code files from your account at http://www. packtpub.com for all the Packt Publishing books you have purchased. If you purchased this book elsewhere, you can visit http://www.packtpub.com/support and register to have the files e-mailed directly to you.

In this console, type $PSVersionTable in the command-line and press *Enter*. If the output is an error message, PowerShell 1.0 is installed, because the $PSVersionTable variable was introduced in PowerShell 2.0. If a table of version information is seen, the PSVersion entry in the table is the installed version. The following is the output on a typical computer, showing that PowerShell 4.0 is installed:

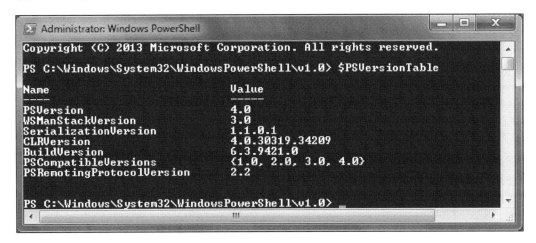

Warning

You might find some references on the Internet telling you to use the get-host cmdlet to easily find the PowerShell version. Unfortunately, this only tells you the version of the PowerShell host, that is, the program you're using to run PowerShell.

Installing/upgrading PowerShell

If you don't have PowerShell installed or want a more recent version of PowerShell, you'll need to find the **Windows Management Framework (WMF)** download that matches the PowerShell version you want. WMF includes PowerShell as well as other related tools such as **Windows Remoting (WinRM)**, **Windows Management Instrumentation (WMI)**, and **Desired State Configuration (DSC)**. The contents of the distribution change from version to version, so make sure to read the release notes included in the download. Here are links to the installers:

PowerShell Version	URL
1.0	http://support.microsoft.com/kb/926139
2.0	http://support2.microsoft.com/kb/968929/en-us
3.0	http://www.microsoft.com/en-us/download/details.aspx?id=34595

PowerShell Version	URL
4.0	`http://www.microsoft.com/en-us/download/details.aspx?id=40855`
5.0 (Feb. Preview)	`http://www.microsoft.com/en-us/download/details.aspx?id=45883`

Note that PowerShell 5.0 has not been officially released, so the table lists the February 2015 preview, the latest at the time of writing.

The PowerShell 1.0 installer was released as an executable (`.exe`), but since then the releases have all been as standalone Windows update installers (`.msu`). All of these are painless to execute. You can simply download the file and run it from the explorer or from the **Run...** option in the start menu. PowerShell installs don't typically require a reboot but it's best to plan on doing one, just in case.

It's important to note that you can only have one version of PowerShell installed, and you can't install a lower version than the version that was shipped with your OS. Also, there are noted compatibility issues between various versions of PowerShell and Microsoft products such as Exchange, System Center, and Small Business Server, so make sure to read the system requirements section on the download page. Most of the conflicts can be resolved with a service pack of the software, but you should be sure of this before upgrading PowerShell on a server.

Starting a PowerShell session

We already started a PowerShell session earlier in the section on using PowerShell to find the installed version. So, what more is there to see? It turns out that there is more than one program used to run PowerShell, possibly more than one version of each of these programs, and finally, more than one way to start each of them. It might sound confusing but it will all make sense shortly.

PowerShell hosts

A PowerShell host is a program that provides access to the PowerShell engine in order to run PowerShell commands and scripts. The `PowerShell.exe` that we saw in the `PSHOME` directory earlier in this chapter is known as the **console host**. It is cosmetically similar to Command Prompt (`cmd.exe`) and only provides a command-line interface. Starting with Version 2.0 of PowerShell, a second host was provided.

The **Integrated Scripting Environment** (ISE) is a graphical environment providing multiple editors in a tabbed interface along with menus and the ability to use plugins. While not as fully featured as an **Integrated Development Environment** (IDE), the ISE is a tremendous productivity tool used to build PowerShell scripts and is a great improvement over using an editor, such as notepad for development.

The ISE executable is stored in PSHOME, and is named powershell_ise.exe. In Version 2.0 of the ISE, there were three sections, a tabbed editor, a console for input, and a section for output. Starting with Version 3.0, the input and output sections were combined into a single console that is more similar to the interface of the console host. The Version 4.0 ISE is shown as follows:

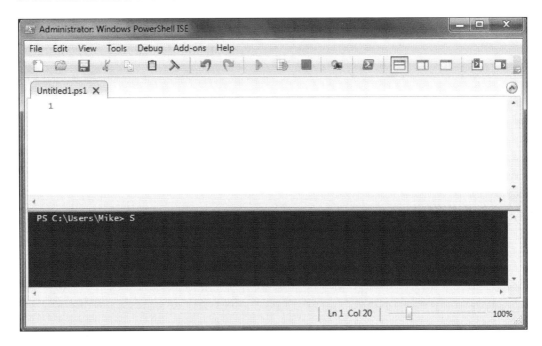

I will be using the **Light Console, Light Editor** theme for the ISE in most of the screenshots for this book, because the dark console does not work well on the printed page. To switch to this theme, open the **Options** item in the **Tools** Menu and select **Manage Themes...** in the options window:

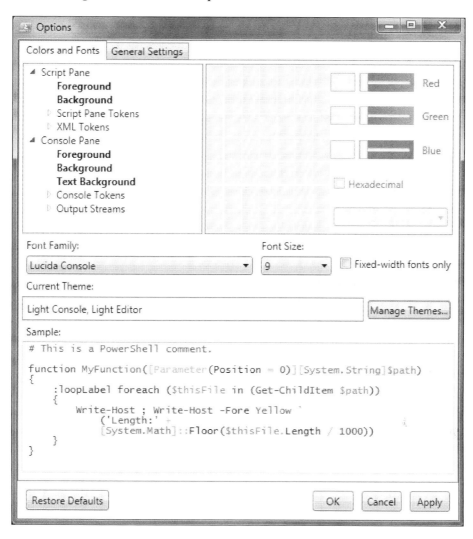

Press the **Manage Themes...** button, select the **Light Console, Light Editor** option from the list and press **OK**. Press **OK** again to exit the options screen and your ISE should look something similar to the following:

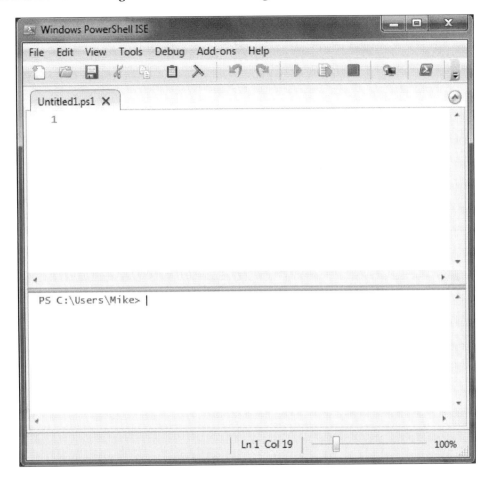

Note that you can customize the appearance of the text in the editor and the console pane in other ways as well. Other than switching to the light console display, I will try to keep the settings to default.

64-bit and 32-bit PowerShell

In addition to the console host and the ISE, if you have a 64-bit operating system, you will also have 64-bit and 32-bit PowerShell installations that will include separate copies of both the hosts.

As mentioned before, the main installation directory, or PSHOME, is found at `%WINDIR%\System32\WindowsPowerShell\v1.0\`. The version of PowerShell in PSHOME matches that of the the operating system. In other words, on a 64-bit OS, the PowerShell in PSHOME is 64-bit. On a 32-bit system, PSHOME has a 32-bit PowerShell install. On a 64-bit system, a second 32-bit system is found in `%WINDIR%\SysWOW64\ WindowsPowerShell\v1.0`.

Isn't that backward?

It seems backward that the 64-bit install is in the `System32` folder and the 32-bit install is in `SysWOW64`. The `System32` folder is always the primary system directory on a Windows computer, and this name has remained for backward compatibility reasons. SysWOW64 is short for Windows on Windows 64-bit. It contains the 32-bit binaries required for 32-bit programs to run in a 64-bit system, since 32-bit programs can't use the 64-bit binaries in System32.

Looking in the `Program Files\Accessories\Windows PowerShell` menu in the start menu of a 64-bit Windows 7 install, we see the following:

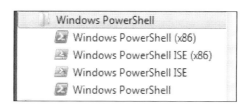

Here, the 32-bit hosts are labeled as (x86) and the 64-bit versions are undesignated. When you run the 32-bit hosts on a 64-bit system, you will also see the (x86) designation in the title bar:

PowerShell as an administrator

When you run a PowerShell host, the session is not elevated. This means that even though you might be an administrator of the machine, the PowerShell session is not running with administrator privileges. This is a safety feature to help prevent users from inadvertently running a script that damages the system.

In order to run a PowerShell session as an administrator, you have a couple of options. First, you can right-click on the shortcut for the host and select **Run as administrator** from the context menu. When you do this, unless you have disabled the UAC alerts, you will see a **User Account Control (UAC)** prompt verifying whether you want to allow the application to run as an administrator.

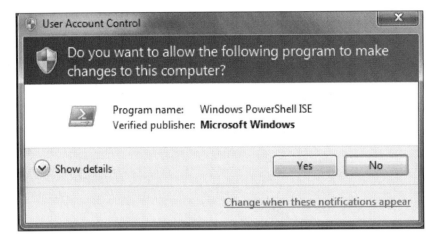

Selecting **Yes** allows the program to run as an administrator, and the title bar reflects that this is the case:

The second way to run one of the hosts as an administrator is to right-click on the shortcut and choose **Properties**. On the shortcut tab of the properties window, press the **Advanced** button. In the **Advanced Properties** window that pops up, check the **Run as administrator** checkbox and press **OK**, and **OK** again to exit out of the properties window:

Using this technique will cause the shortcut to always launch as an administrator, although the UAC prompt will still appear.

> If you choose to disable UAC, PowerShell hosts always run as administrators. Note that disabling UAC alerts is not recommended.

Simple PowerShell commands

Now that we know all the ways that can get a PowerShell session started, what can we do in a PowerShell session? I like to introduce people to PowerShell by pointing out that most of the command-line tools that they already know work fine in PowerShell. For instance, try using DIR, CD, IPCONFIG, and PING. Commands that are part of Command Prompt (think DOS commands) might work slightly different in PowerShell if you look closely, but typical command-line applications work exactly the same as they have always worked in Command Prompt:

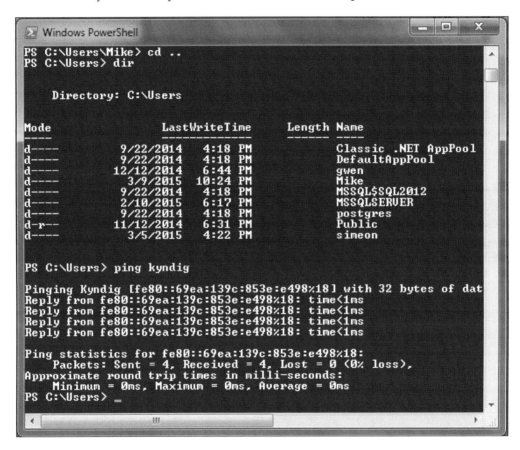

PowerShell commands, called cmdlets, are named with a verb-noun convention. Approved verbs come from a list maintained by Microsoft and can be displayed using the get-verb cmdlet:

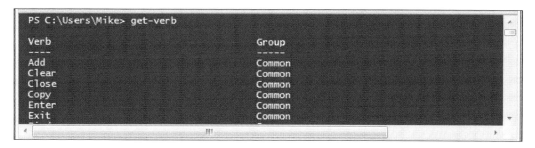

```
PS C:\Users\Mike> get-verb

Verb                                    Group
----                                    -----
Add                                     Common
Clear                                   Common
Close                                   Common
Copy                                    Common
Enter                                   Common
Exit                                    Common
```

By controlling the list of verbs, Microsoft has made it easier to learn PowerShell. The list is not very long and it doesn't contain verbs that have the same meaning (such as Stop, End, Terminate, and Quit), so once you learn a cmdlet using a specific verb, you can easily guess the meaning of the cmdlet names that include the verb.

Some other easy to understand cmdlets are:

- Clear-Host (clears the screen)
- Get-Date (outputs the date)
- Start-Service (starts a service)
- Stop-Process (stops a process)
- Get-Help (shows help about something)

Note that these use several different verbs. From this list, you can probably guess what cmdlet you would use to stop a service. Since you know there's a Start-Service cmdlet, and you know from the Stop-Process cmdlet that Stop is a valid verb, it is logical that Stop-Service is what you would use. The consistency of PowerShell cmdlet naming is a tremendous benefit to learners of PowerShell, and it is a policy that is important as you write the PowerShell code.

What is a cmdlet?

The term cmdlet was coined by Jeffery Snover, the inventor of PowerShell to refer to the PowerShell commands. The PowerShell commands aren't particularly different from other commands, but by giving a unique name to them, he ensured that PowerShell users would be able to use search engines to easily find PowerShell code simply by including the term cmdlet.

PowerShell aliases

If you tried to use DIR and CD in the last section, you may have noticed that they didn't work exactly as the DOS commands that they resemble. In case you didn't see this, enter DIR /S on a PowerShell prompt and see what happens. You will either get an error complaining about a path not existing, or get a listing of a directory called S. Either way, it's not the listing of files including subdirectories. Similarly, you might have noticed that CD in PowerShell allows you to switch between drives without using the /D option and even lets you change to a UNC path. The point is that, these are not DOS commands. What you're seeing is a PowerShell **alias**.

Aliases in PowerShell are alternate names that PowerShell uses for both PowerShell commands and programs. For instance, in PowerShell, DIR is actually an alias for the Get-ChildItem cmdlet. The CD alias points to the Set-Location cmdlet. Aliases exist for many of the cmdlets that perform operations similar to the commands in DOS, Linux, or Unix shells. Aliases serve two main purposes in PowerShell, as follows:

- They allow more concise code on Command Prompt
- They ease users' transition from other shells to PowerShell

To see a list of all the aliases defined in PowerShell, you can use the Get-Alias cmdlet. To find what an alias references, type Get-Alias <alias>. For example, see the following screenshot:

To find out what aliases exist for a cmdlet, type Get-Alias -Definition <cmdlet> as follows:

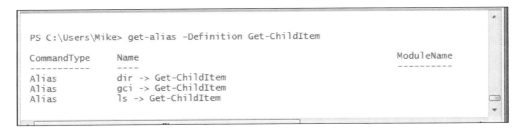

Here we can see that the `Get-ChildItem` cmdlet has three aliases. The first and last assist in transitioning from DOS and Linux shells, and the middle one is an abbreviation using the first letters in the name of the cmdlet.

Summary

This chapter focused on figuring out what version of PowerShell was installed and the many ways to start a PowerShell session. A quick introduction to PowerShell cmdlets showed that a lot of the command-line knowledge we have from DOS can be used in PowerShell and that aliases make this transition easier.

In the next chapter, we will look at the `Get-Command`, `Get-Help`, and `Get-Member` cmdlets, and learn how they unlock the entire PowerShell ecosystem for us.

For further reading

The Monad Manifesto, which outlines the original vision of the PowerShell project: `http://blogs.msdn.com/b/powershell/archive/2007/03/19/monad-manifesto-the-origin-of-windows-powershell.aspx`

Microsoft's approved cmdlet verb list: `http://msdn.microsoft.com/en-us/library/ms714428.aspx`

- `get-help about_aliases`
- `get-help about_PowerShell.exe`
- `get-help about_ PowerShell_ISE.exe`

2
Building Blocks

Even though books, videos, and the Internet can be helpful in your efforts to learn PowerShell, you will find that your greatest ally in this quest is PowerShell itself. In this chapter, we will look at two fundamental weapons in any PowerShell scripter's arsenal, the `Get-Command` and `Get-Help` cmdlets. The topics covered in this chapter include the following:

- Finding commands using `Get-Command`
- Finding commands using tab completion
- Using `Get-Help` to understand cmdlets
- Interpreting the command syntax

What can you do?

You saw in the previous chapter that you are able to run standard command-line programs in PowerShell and that there are aliases defined for some cmdlets that allow you to use the names of commands that you are used to from other shells. Other than these, what can you use? How do you know which commands, cmdlets, and aliases are available?

The answer is the first of the **big three** cmdlets, the Get-Command cmdlet. Simply executing Get-Command with no parameters displays a list of all the entities that PowerShell considers to be executable. This includes programs in the path (the environment variable), cmdlets, functions, scripts, and aliases.

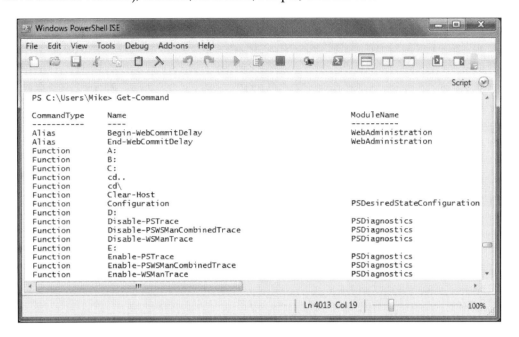

This list of commands is long and gets longer with each new operating system and PowerShell release. To count the output, we can use this command:

```
Get-Command | Measure-Object
```

The output of this command is as follows:

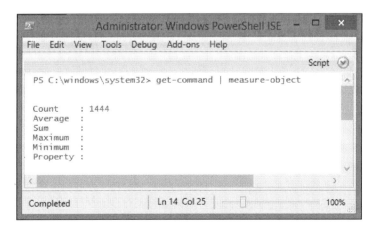

The pipe character (|) tells PowerShell to use the output of the command on the left of the pipe as the input of the command on the right. In this example, it says that the output of the get-command cmdlet should be used as the input for the measure-object cmdlet.

The Measure-Object cmdlet can be used to count the number of items in the output from a command. In this case, it tells us that there are 1444 different commands available to us. In the output, we can see that there is a CommandType column. There is a corresponding parameter to the Get-Command cmdlet that allows us to filter the output and only shows us certain kinds of commands. Limiting the output to the cmdlets shows that there are 706 different cmdlets available:

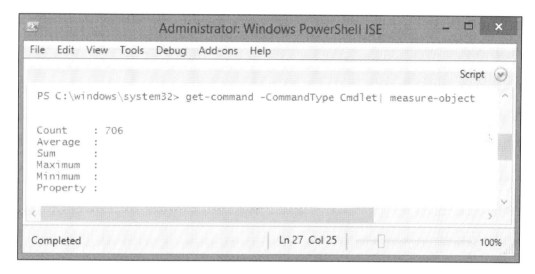

Getting a big list such as this isn't very useful though. In reality, you are usually going to use Get-Command to find commands that pertain to a component you want to work with. For instance, if you need to work with Windows services, you could issue a command such as Get-Command *Service* using wildcards to include any command that includes the word service in its name. The output would look something similar to the following:

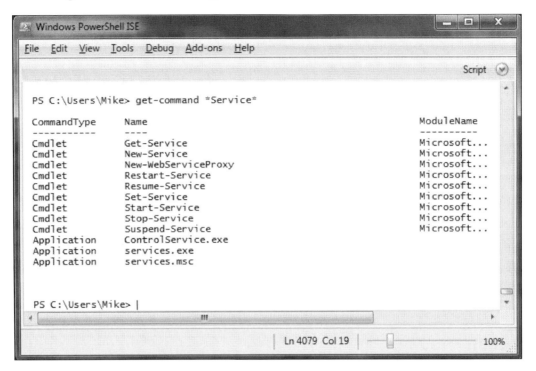

You can see in the output that applications found in the current path and the PowerShell cmdlets are both included. Unfortunately, there's also a cmdlet called New-WebServiceProxy, which clearly doesn't have anything to do with Windows services. To better control the matching of cmdlets with your subject, you can use the –Noun parameter to filter the commands. Note that by naming a noun, you are implicitly limiting the results to PowerShell objects because nouns are a PowerShell concept. Using this approach gives us a smaller list:

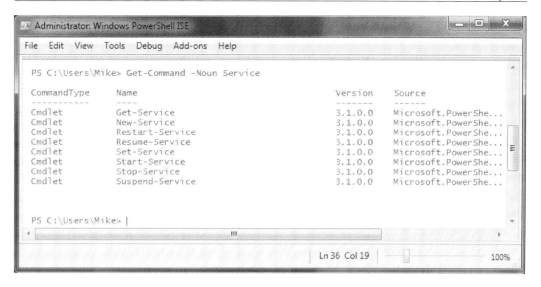

The scripter's secret weapon – tab completion

Although Get-Command is a great way to find cmdlets, the truth is that the PowerShell cmdlet names are very predictable. In fact, they're so predictable that after you've been using PowerShell for a while you won't probably turn to Get-Command very often. After you've found the noun or the set of nouns that you're working with, the powerful tab completion found in both the PowerShell console and the ISE will allow you to enter just a part of the command and press *tab* to cycle through the list of commands that match what you have entered. For instance, in keeping with our examples dealing with services, you could enter *-Service at the command line and press *tab*. You would first see **Get-Service**, followed by the rest of the items in the previous screenshot as you hit *tab*. Tab completion is a huge benefit for your scripting productivity for several reasons, such as:

- You get the suggestions where you need them
- The suggestions are all valid command names
- The suggestions are consistently capitalized

In addition to being able to complete the command names, tab completion also gives suggestions for parameter names, property, and method names, and in PowerShell 3.0 and above, it gives the parameter values. The combination of tab completion improvements and IntelliSense in the ISE is so impressive that I recommend that people upgrade their development workstation to at least PowerShell 3.0, even if they are developing PowerShell code that will run in a 2.0 environment.

How does that work?

Knowing what commands you can execute is a big step, but it doesn't help much if you don't know how you can use them. Again, PowerShell is here to help you. To see a quick hint of how to use a cmdlet, write the cmdlet name followed by -?. The beginning of this output for Get-Service is shown as follows:

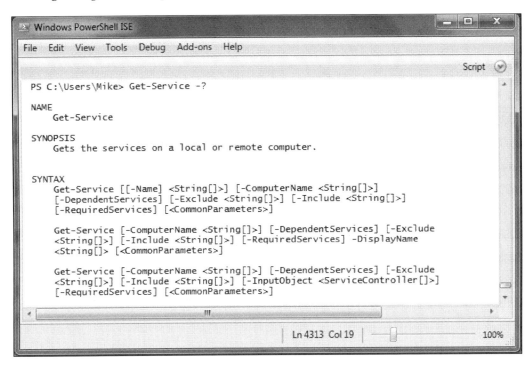

Even this brief help, which was truncated to fit on the page, shows a brief synopsis of the cmdlet and the syntax to call it, including the possible parameters and their types. The rest of the display shows a longer description of the cmdlet, a list of the related topics, and some instructions about getting more help about Get-Service:

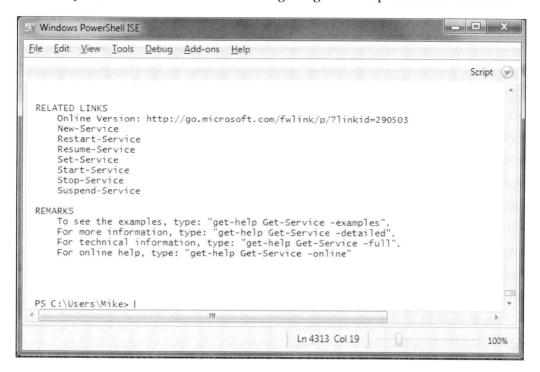

In the **Remarks** section, we can see that there's a cmdlet called `Get-Help` (the second of the "big 3" cmdlets) that allows us to view more extensive help in PowerShell. The first type of extra help we can see is the examples. The example output begins with the name and synopsis of the cmdlet and is followed, in the case of `Get-Service`, by 11 examples that range from simple to complex. The help for each cmdlet is different, but in general you will find these examples to be a treasure trove providing an insight into not only how the cmdlets behave in isolation, but also in combination with other commands in real scenarios:

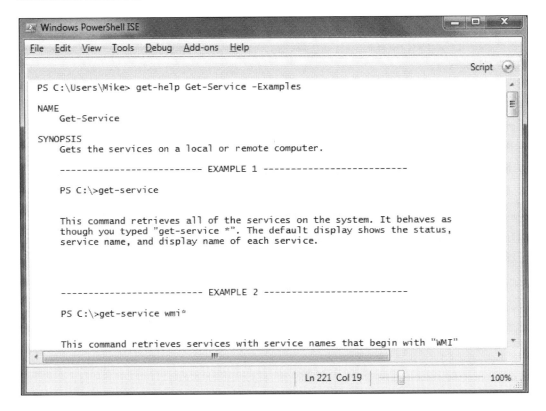

Also, mentioned in this are the ways to display more information about the cmdlet using the `-Detailed` or `-Full` switches with `Get-Help`. The `-Detailed` switch shows the examples as well as the basic descriptions of each parameter. The `-Full` switch adds sections on inputs, outputs, and detailed parameter information to the `-Detailed` output.

 Using `Get-Help` for a cmdlet without specifying any other parameters gives the same output as using `-?` after the cmdlet name.

If you're running PowerShell 3.0 or above, instead of getting a complete help entry, you probably received a message like this:

```
REMARKS
    To get the latest Help content including descriptions
    and examples type: Update-Help.
```

This is because in PowerShell 3.0, the PowerShell team switched to the concept of update-able help. In order to deal with time constraints around shipping and the complexity of releasing updates to installed software, the help content for the PowerShell modules is now updated via a cmdlet called `Update-Help`. Using this mechanism, the team can revise, expand, and correct the help content on a continual basis, and users can be sure to have the most recent content at all times:

 Update-Help requires an elevated session, so make sure that you start the PowerShell session as an administrator before trying to update your help content.

In addition to the help with individual cmdlets, PowerShell includes help content about all aspects of the PowerShell environment. These help topics are named beginning with `about_` and can also be viewed with the `Get-Help` cmdlet. The list of topics can be retrieved using `get-Help about_*`:

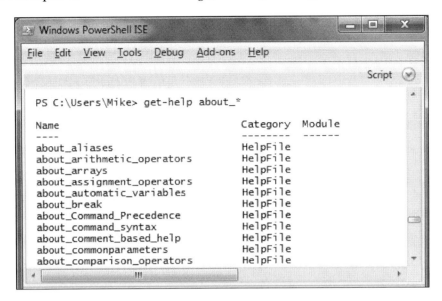

Using `measure-object`, as we saw in a previous section, we can see that there are 124 topics listed in my installation:

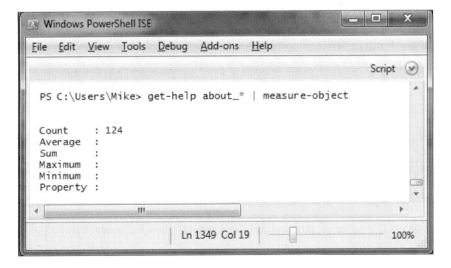

These help topics are often extremely long and contain some of the best documentation on the working of PowerShell you will ever find. For that reason, I will end each chapter in this book with a list of help topics to read about the topics covered in the chapter.

In addition to reading the help content in the output area of the ISE and the text console, PowerShell 3.0 added a -ShowWindow switch to get-help that allows viewing in a separate window. All help content is shown in the window, but sections can be hidden using the settings button:

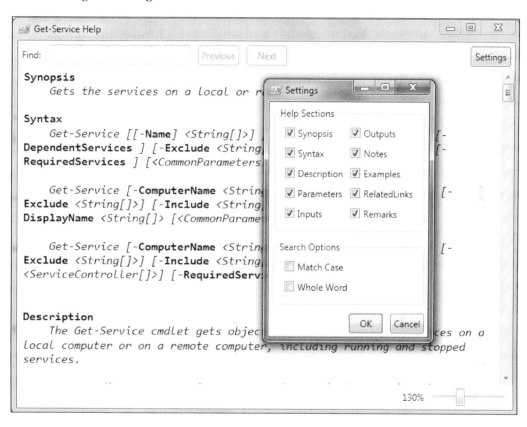

Interpreting the cmdlet syntax

The syntax section of the cmdlet help can be overwhelming at first, so let's drill into it a bit and try to understand it in detail. I will use the get-service cmdlet for an example, but the principles are same for any cmdlet:

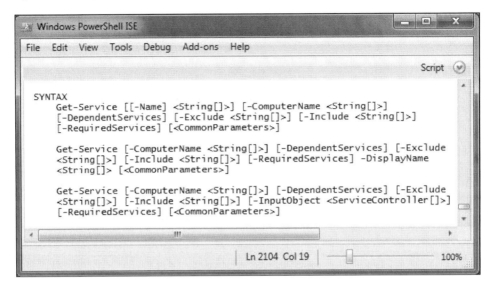

The first thing to notice is that there are three different get-service calls illustrated here. They correspond to the PowerShell concept of **ParameterSets**, but you can think of them as different use cases for the cmdlet. Each ParameterSet, or use case will have at least one unique parameter. In this case, the first includes the –Name parameter, the second includes –DisplayName, and the third has the –InputObject parameter.

Each ParameterSet lists the parameters that can be used in a particular scenario. The way the parameter is shown in the listing, tells you how the parameter can be used. For instance, [[-Name] <String[]>] means that the name parameter has the following attributes:

- It is optional (because the whole definition is in brackets)
- The parameter name can be omitted (because the name is in brackets)
- The parameter values can be an array (list) of strings (String[])

Many cmdlet parameters allow lists to be passed, rather than only a single value. Taking the time to check the types of parameters can make it simpler and quicker to write scripts, if you can eliminate looping because you are able to pass all the values at once.

In general, a parameter will be shown in one of the following forms:

Form	Meaning
`[[-Param] T]`	Optional parameter of type `T` with the name optional
`[-Param T]`	Optional parameter of type `T` with the name required
`-Param T`	Required parameter of type `T`
`[-Param]`	A switch (flag)

Applying this to the `Get-Service` syntax shown previously, we see that some valid calls of the cmdlet could be:

- `Get-Service WinRM`

- `Get-Service –Name WinRM`

- `Get-Service *SQL* -Exclude SQLWriter`

- `Get-Service aspnet_state,W3SVC`

Your turn!

Read the `help` for another cmdlet (`get-process` is a good candidate) and work through the syntax until you understand how the parameters are specified.

Summary

This chapter dealt with the first two of the "big three" cmdlets for learning PowerShell, `get-Command` and `get-Help`. These two cmdlets allow you to find out which commands are available and how to use them. In the next chapter, we will finish the "big 3" with the `get-member` cmdlet that will help us to figure out what to do with the output we receive.

For further reading

- `Get-Help Get-Command`

- `Get-Help Get-Help`

- `Get-Help Get-Member`

- `Get-Help about_Updateable_Help`

- `Get-Help Update-Help`

- `Get-Help about_Command_Syntax`

3
Objects and PowerShell

In this chapter, we will learn about objects and how they relate to the PowerShell output. The specific topics in this chapter include the following:

- What are objects?
- Comparing DOS and PowerShell output
- The `Get-Member` cmdlet

Objects all the way down

One major difference between PowerShell and other command environments is that, in PowerShell, everything is an object. One result of this is that the output from the PowerShell cmdlets is always in the form of objects. Before we look at how this affects PowerShell, let's take some time to understand what we mean when we talk about objects.

Digging into objects

If everything is an object, it's probably worth taking a few minutes to talk about what this means. We don't have to be experts in object-oriented programming to work in PowerShell, but a knowledge of a few things is necessary.

In a nutshell, object-oriented programming involves encapsulating the related values and functionality in objects. For instance, instead of having variables for speed, height, and direction and a function called PLOTPROJECTILE, in object-oriented programming you might have a Projectile object that has the properties called `Speed`, `Height`, and `Direction` as well as a method called `Plot`. This Projectile object could be treated as a single unit and passed as a parameter to other functions. Keeping the values and the related code together has a certain sense to it, and there are many other benefits to object-oriented programming.

Types, classes, and objects

The main concepts in object-oriented programming are types, classes, and objects. These concepts are all related and often confusing, but not difficult once you have them straight:

- A **type** is an abstract representation of structured data combining values (called properties), code (called methods), and behavior (called events). These attributes are collectively known as **members**.

- A **class** is a specific implementation of one or more types. As such, it will contain all the members that are specified in each of these types and possibly other members as well. In some languages, a class is also considered a type. This is the case in C#.

- An **object** is a specific instance of a class. Most of the time in PowerShell, we will be working with objects. As mentioned earlier, all output in PowerShell is in the form of objects.

PowerShell is build upon the .NET framework, so we will be referring to the .NET framework throughout this book. In the .NET framework, there is a type called `System.IO.FileSystemInfo`, which describes the items located in a filesystem (of course). Two classes that implement this type are `System.IO.FileInfo` and `System.IO.DirectoryInfo`. A reference to a specific file would be an object that was an instance of the `System.IO.FileInfo` class. The object would also be considered to be of the `System.IO.FileSystemInfo` and `System.IO.FileInfo` types.

Here are some other examples that should help make things clear:

- All the objects in the .NET ecosystem are of the `System.Object` type
- Many collections in .NET are of the `IEnumerable` type
- The ArrayList is of the `IList` and `ICollection` types among others

What are members?

Members are the attributes of types that are implemented in classes and instantiated in objects. Members come in many forms in the .NET framework, including properties, methods, and events.

Properties represent the data contained in an object. For instance, in a `FileInfo` object (`System.IO.FileInfo`), there would be properties referring to the filename, file extension, length, and various `DateTime` values associated with the file. An object referring to a service (of the `System.ServiceProcess.ServiceController` type) would have properties for the display name of the service and the state (running or not).

Methods refer to the operations that the objects (or sometimes classes) can perform. A service object, for instance, can Start and Stop. A database command object can Execute. A file object can Delete or Encrypt itself. Most objects have some methods (for example, `ToString` and `Equals`) because they are of the `System.Object` type.

Events are a way for an object to notify that something has happened or that a condition has been met. Button objects, for instance, have an `OnClick` event that is triggered when they are clicked.

Now that we have an idea about objects, let's look back at a couple of familiar DOS commands and see how they deal with the output.

The DOS DIR command

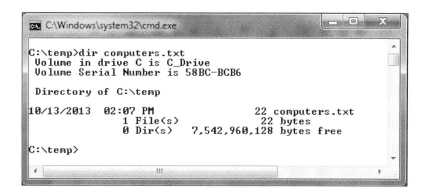

The output that we see in the preceding screenshot includes several details about a single file. Note that there is a lot of formatting included with the static text (for example, `Volume in drive`) and some tabular information, but the only way to get to these details is to understand exactly how the output is formatted and parse the output string accordingly. Think about how the output would change, if there were more than one file listed. If we included the /S switch, the output would have spanned over multiple directories, and would have been broken into sections accordingly. Finding a specific piece of information from this is not a trivial operation, and the process of retrieving the file length, for example, would be different from how you would go about retrieving the file extension.

The IPCONFIG command

Another command that we are all familiar with is the IPConfig.exe tool, which shows network adapter information. Here is the beginning of the output in my laptop:

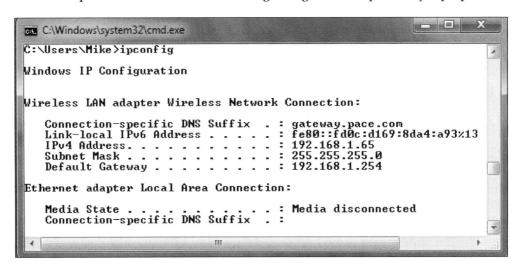

Here, again, the output is very mixed. There is a lot of static text and a list of properties and values. The property names are very readable, which is nice for humans, but not so nice for computers trying to parse things out. The dot-leaders are again something that help to guide the eyes towards the property values, but will get in the way when we try to parse out the values that we are looking for. Since some of the values (such as IP addresses and subnet masks) already include dots, I imagine it will cause some confusion.

PowerShell for comparison

Let's look at some PowerShell commands and compare how easy it is to get what we need out of the output:

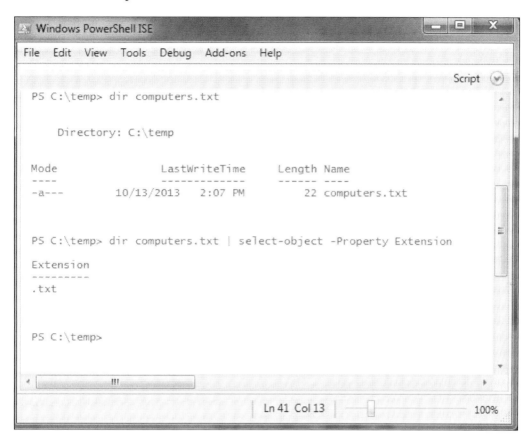

We can see that the output of the `dir` command looks similar to the output we saw in DOS, but we can follow this with `Select-Object` to pull out a specific property. This is possible because PowerShell commands always output objects. In this case, the object in question has a property called `Extension`, which we can inspect. We will talk about the `select-object` cmdlet in detail in the next chapter, but for now it is enough to know that it can be used to limit the output to a specific set of properties from the original objects.

The Get-Member cmdlet

One way to find the members of a class is to look up this class online in the **MicroSoft Developers Network (MSDN)**. For instance, the `FileInfo` class is found at `https://msdn.microsoft.com/en-us/library/system.io.fileinfo`.

Although this is a good reference, it's not very handy to switch back and forth between PowerShell and a browser to look at the classes all the time. Fortunately, PowerShell has a very handy way to give this information, the `Get-Member` cmdlet. This is the third of the "big 3" cmdlets, following `Get-Command` and `Get-Help`.

The most common way to use the `Get-Member` cmdlet is to **pipe** data into it. Piping is a way to pass data from one cmdlet to another, and is covered in depth in the next chapter. Using a pipe with `Get-Member` looks like this:

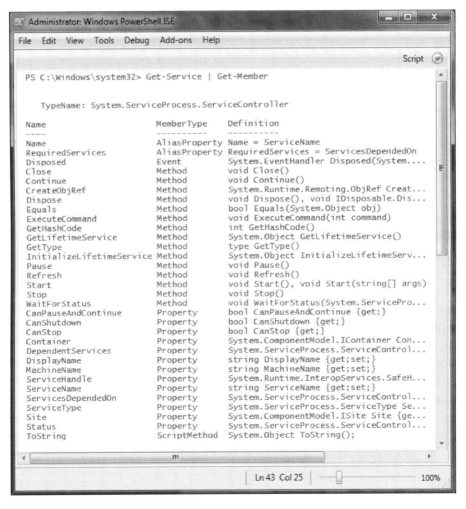

The `Get-Member` cmdlet looks at all the objects in its input, and provides output for each distinct class. In this output, we can see that `Get-Service` only outputs a single type, `System.ServiceProcess.ServiceController`. The name of the class is followed by the list of members, type of each member as well as definition for the member. The member definition shows the type of properties, signature for events, and methods, which includes the return type as well as the types of parameters.

Your turn!

Use `Get-Member` to see the classes output by the `Dir` (or `Get-ChildItem`) cmdlet. Note that there are two different classes listed.

One thing that can be confusing is that `get-member` usually shows more properties than those shown in the output. For instance, the `Get-Member` output for the previous `Get-Service` cmdlet shows 13 properties but the output of `Get-Service` displays only three.

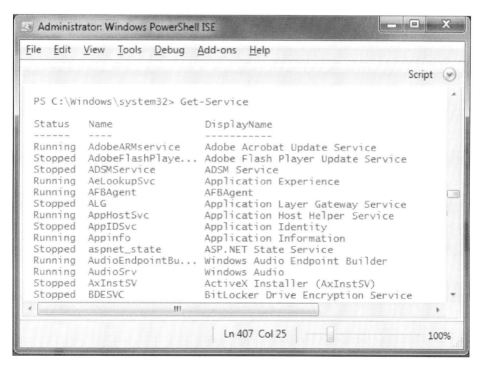

The reason for this is that PowerShell has a powerful formatting system that is configured with some default formats for familiar objects. Rest assured that all the properties are there. A couple of quick ways to see all the properties are to use the Select-Object cmdlet we saw earlier in this chapter or to use the Format-List cmdlet and force all the properties to be shown. Here, we use Select-Object and a wildcard to specify all the properties:

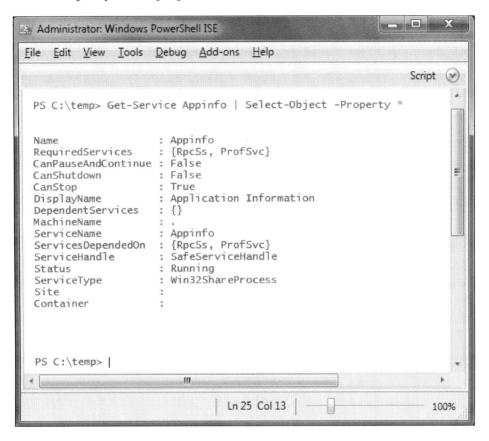

The Format-List cmdlet with a wildcard for properties gives output that looks the same . We will discuss how the output of these two cmdlets actually differs, as well as elaborate on PowerShell's formatting system in *Chapter 5, Formatting Output*.

Where did these all come from?

If you look closely at the ServiceController members listed in the previous figure, you will notice a few members that aren't strictly properties, methods, or events. PowerShell has a mechanism called the Extended Type System that allows PowerShell to add members to classes or to individual objects. In the case of the SystemController objects, PowerShell adds a Name alias for the ServiceName property and a RequiredServices alias for the built-in ServicesDependedOn property.

Your turn!

Use Get-Member with Dir and Get-Process and see what members PowerShell has added. Look these classes up on MSDN and verify that those properties aren't delivered as part of the .NET framework.

Summary

In this chapter, we discussed the importance of objects as output from the PowerShell cmdlets. After a brief primer on types, classes, and objects, we spent some time getting used to the Get-Member cmdlet. In the next chapter, we will cover the PowerShell pipeline and common pipeline cmdlets.

For further reading

- Get-Help about_objects
- Get-Help about_properties
- Get-Help about_methods
- Get-Help about_events
- Get-Help Get-Member

4
Life on the Assembly Line

The object-oriented pipeline is one of the distinctive features of the PowerShell environment. The ability to refer to properties of arbitrary objects without parsing increases the expressiveness of the language and allows you to work with all kinds of objects with ease.

In this chapter, we will cover the following topics:

- How the pipeline works
- Some of the most common cmdlets to deal with data on the pipeline:
    - `Sort-Object`
    - `Where-Object`
    - `Select-Object`
    - `Group-Object`

The pipeline as an assembly line

The pipeline in PowerShell is a mechanism to get data from one command to another. Simply put, the data that is output from the first command is treated as input to the next command in the pipeline. The pipeline isn't limited to two commands, though. It can be extended practically as long as you like, although readability would suffer if the line got too long.

Here is a simple pipeline example:

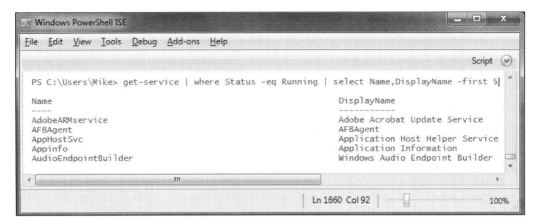

In this example, I've used some common aliases for cmdlets (`where`, `select`) to keep the line from wrapping. I'll try to include aliases when I mention cmdlets, but if you can't figure out what a command is referring to, remember you can always use `Get-Command` to find out what is going on. For example, `Get-Command where` tells you `Where` is an alias for `Where-Object`. In this case, `select` is an alias for `Select-Object`.

The execution of this pipeline can be thought of in the following sequence:

- Get the list of services
- Choose the services that have the `Running` status
- Select the first five services
- Output the **Name** and **Display Name** of each one

Even though this is a single line, it shows some of the power of PowerShell. The line is very expressive, doesn't include a lot of extra syntactic baggage, and doesn't even require any variables. It also doesn't use explicit types or loops. It is a very unexceptional bit of PowerShell code, but this single line represents logic that would take several lines of code in a traditional language to express.

This isn't your DOS or Linux pipeline

DOS and Linux (and Unix, for that matter) have had pipes for a long time. Pipes in these systems work similar to how PowerShell pipes work on one level. In all of them, output is streamed from one command to the next. In other shells, though, the data being passed is simple, flat text.

For a command to use the text, it either needs to parse the text to get to the interesting bits, or it needs to treat the entire output like a blob. Since Linux and Unix use text-based configurations for most operating system functions, this makes sense. A wide range of tools to parse and find substrings is available in these systems, and scripting can be very complex.

Objects at your disposal

In Windows, however, there aren't a lot of text-based configurations. Most components are managed using the Win32 or .NET APIs. PowerShell is built upon the .NET framework and leverages the .NET object model instead of using text as the primary focus. As data in the pipeline is always in the form objects, you rarely need to parse it and can directly deal with the properties of the objects themselves. As long as the properties are named reasonably (and they usually are), you will be able to quickly get to the data you need.

Dealing with pipeline data

Since commands on the pipeline have access to object properties, several general-purpose cmdlets exist to perform common operations. Since these cmdlets can work with any kind of object, they use Object as the noun (you remember the Verb-Noun naming convention for cmdlets, right?).

To find the list of these cmdlets, we can use the Get-Command cmdlet:

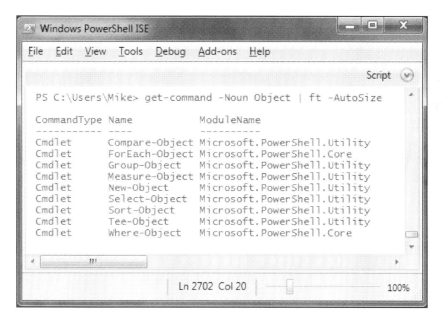

ft is an alias for the `Format-Table` cmdlet, which I'm using here to get the display to fit more nicely on the screen. It will be covered in depth in *Chapter 5, Formatting Output*.

The `Sort-Object`, `Select-Object`, and `Where-Object` cmdlets are some of the most used cmdlets in PowerShell.

The Sort-Object cmdlet

Sorting data can be interesting. Have you ever sorted a list of numbers only to find that 11 came between 1 and 2? That's because the sort that you used treated the numbers as text. Sorting dates with all the different culture-specific formatting can also be a challenge. Fortunately, PowerShell handles sorting details for you with the `Sort-Object` cmdlet.

Let's look at a few examples of the `Sort-Object` cmdlet before getting into the details. We'll start by sorting a directory listing by length:

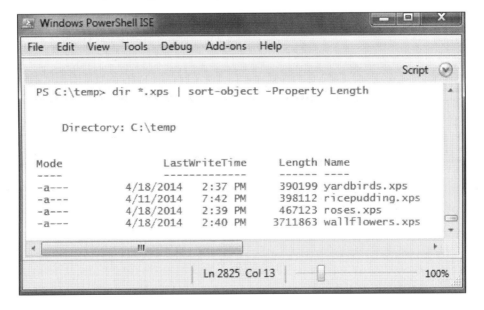

Sorting this in reverse isn't difficult either.

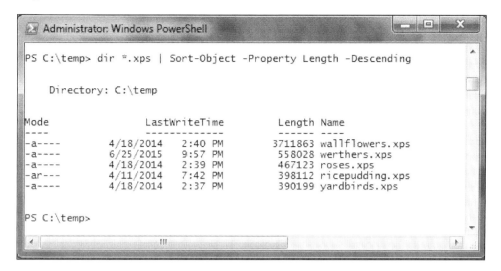

Sorting by more than one property is a breeze as well. Here, I omitted the parameter name (`-Property`) to shorten the command-line a bit:

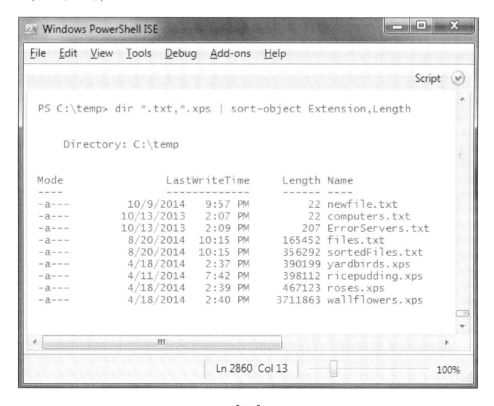

You try it!

Use the Sort-object cmdlet in conjunction with dir (Get-ChildItem), Get-Service, or Get-Process. Try sorting by more than one property or in reverse. Note that the dates and numbers are sorted correctly, even though the text might not be alphabetically sorted.

Looking at the brief help for the Sort-Object cmdlet, we can see a few other parameters, such as:

- -Unique (return distinct items found in the input)
- -CaseSensitive (force a case-sensitive sort)
- -Culture (specify what culture to use while sorting)

As it turns out, you will probably find few occasions to use these parameters and will be fine with the -Property and -Descending parameters.

The Where-Object cmdlet

Another cmdlet that is extremely useful is the **Where-Object** cmdlet. Where-Object is used to filter the pipeline data based on a condition that is tested for each item in the pipeline. Any object in the pipeline that causes the condition to evaluate to a true value is output from the Where-Object cmdlet. Objects that cause the condition to evaluate to a false value are not passed on as output.

For instance, we might want to find all the files that are below 100 bytes in size in the c:\temp directory. One way to do that is to use the simplified, or comparison syntax for Where-Object, which was introduced in PowerShell 3.0. In this syntax, the command would look like this:

```
Dir c:\temp | Where-Object Length –lt 100
```

In this syntax, we can compare a single property of each object with a constant value. The comparison operator here is -lt, which is how PowerShell expresses "less than".

All PowerShell comparison operators start with a dash. This can be confusing, but the < and > symbols have an entrenched meaning in shells, so they can't be used as operators. Common operators include -eq, -ne, -lt, -gt, -le, -ge, -not, and -like. For a full list of operators, try get-help about_operators.

If you need to use PowerShell 1.0 or 2.0, or need to specify a condition more complex than it is allowed in the simplified syntax, you can use the general or **scriptblock** syntax. Expressing the same condition using this form looks as follows:

```
Dir c:\temp | Where-Object {$_.Length -lt 100}
```

This looks a lot more complicated, but it's not so bad. The construction in curly braces is called a scriptblock, and is simply a block of the PowerShell code. In the scriptblock syntax, $_ stands for the current object in the pipeline and we're referencing the **Length** property of that object using dot-notation. The good thing about the general syntax of Where-Object is that we can do more inside the scriptblock than simply test one condition. For instance, we could check for files below 100 bytes or those that were created after 1/1/2015, as follows:

```
Dir c:\temp | Where-Object {$_.Length -lt 100 -or $_.CreationTime -gt
'1/1/2015'}
```

Here's this command running on my laptop:

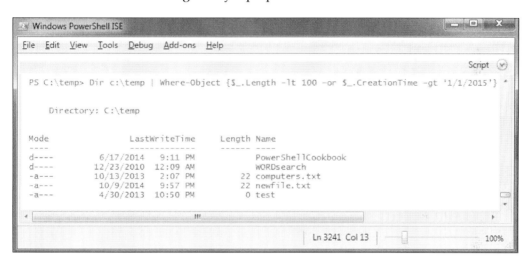

If you're using PowerShell 3.0 or above and need to use the scriptblock syntax, you can substitute $_ with $PSItem in the scriptblock. The meaning is the same and $PSItem is a bit more readable. It makes the line slightly longer, but it's a small sacrifice to make for readability's sake.

The examples that I've shown so far, have used simple comparisons with properties, but in the scriptblock syntax, any condition can be included. Also, note that any value other than a logical false value (expressed by `$false` in PowerShell), `0`, or an empty string (") is considered to be true (`$true`) in PowerShell. So, for example, we could filter objects using the `Get-Member` cmdlet to only show objects that have a particular property, as follows:

```
Dir | where-object {$_ | get-member Length}
```

This will return all objects in the current directory that have a `Length` property. Since files have lengths and directories don't, this is one way to get a list of files and omit the subdirectories.

You try it!
Use the `Where-Object` cmdlet to find all of the `*.ps*` files in `$PSHOME` that are larger than 1 kilobyte in size. Remember that you can express 1kilobyte using the KB unit suffix (1KB).

The Select-Object cmdlet

The **Select-Object** cmdlet is a versatile cmdlet that you will find yourself using often. There are three main ways that it is used:

- Limiting the number of the objects returned
- Limiting the properties of the objects returned
- Retrieving the value of a single property of the objects in the pipeline

Limiting the number of objects returned

Sometimes, you just want to see a few of the objects that are in the pipeline. To accomplish this, you can use the `-First`, `-Last`, and `-Skip` parameters. The `-First` parameter indicates that you want to see a particular number of objects from the beginning of the list of objects in the pipeline. Similarly, the `-Last` parameter selects objects from the end of the list of objects in the pipeline.

For instance, getting the first two processes in the list from Get-Process is simple:

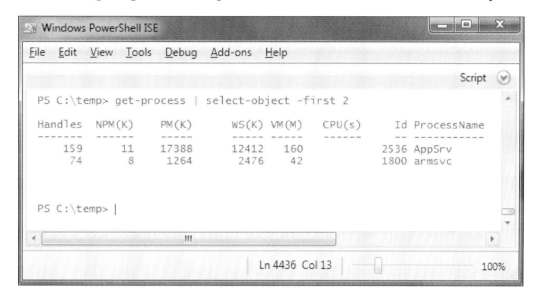

Since we didn't use Sort-Object to force the order of the objects in the pipeline, we don't know that these are the first alphabetically, but they were the first two that were output from Get-Process.

You can use –Skip to cause a certain number of objects to be bypassed before returning the objects. It can be used by itself to output the rest of the objects after the skipped ones, or in conjunction with –First or –Last to return all but the beginning or end of the list of objects. As an example, -Skip can be used to skip over header lines when reading a file using the Get-Content cmdlet.

Limiting the properties of the objects returned

Sometimes, the objects in the pipeline have more properties than you need. To select only certain properties from the list of objects in the pipeline, you can use the −Property parameter with a list of properties. For instance, to get only the Name, Extension, and Length from the directory listing, you could do something like this:

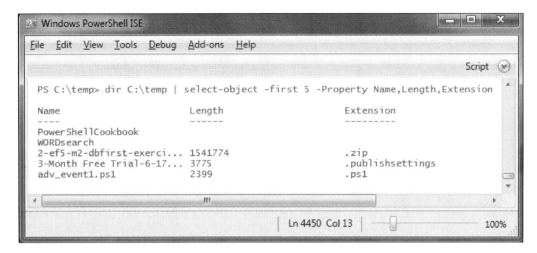

I used the −First parameter as well to save some space in the output, but the important thing is that we only got the three properties that we asked for.

Note that, here, the first two objects in the pipeline were directories, and directory objects don't have a length property. PowerShell provides an empty value of $null for missing properties like this. Also, note that these objects weren't formatted like a directory listing. We'll talk about formatting in detail in the next chapter, but for now, you should just know that these limited objects are not of the same type as the original objects, so the formatting system treated them differently.

You try it!
Use the Get-Member cmdlet to verify that the type of the objects change slightly when you use the −Property parameter of Select-Object.

Retrieving the values of a single property

Sometimes, you want to get the values of a single property of a set of objects. For instance, if you wanted to get the display names of all of the services installed on your computer, you might try to do something like this:

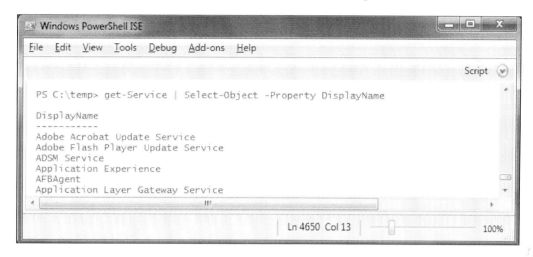

This is close to what you were looking for, but instead of getting a bunch of names (strings), you got a bunch of objects with the DisplayName properties. A hint that this is what happened is seen by the heading (and underline) of DisplayName. You can also verify this using the Get-Member cmdlet:

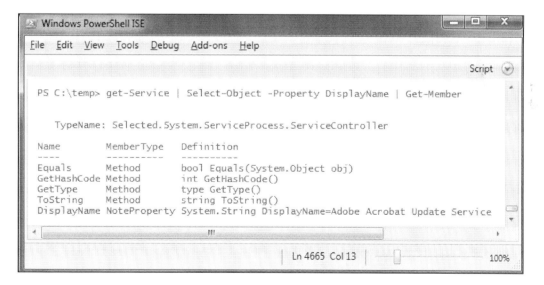

In order to just get the values and not objects, you need to use the -ExpandProperty parameter. Unlike the -Property parameter, you can only specify a single property with -ExpandProperty, and the output is a list of raw values. Notice that with -ExpandProperty, the column heading is gone:

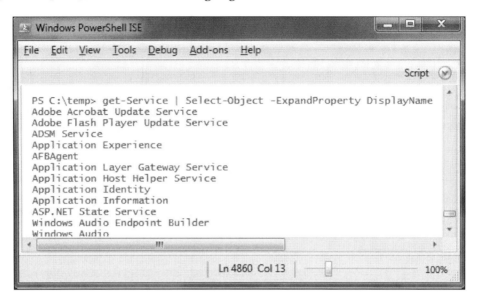

We can also verify using Get-Member that we just got strings instead of objects with a DisplayName property:

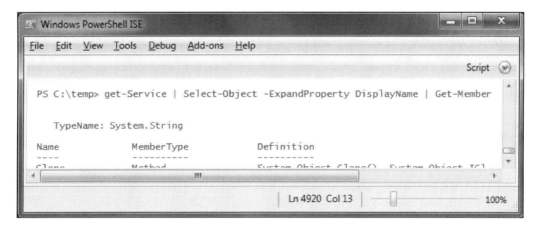

There are a few other parameters for Select-Object, but they will be less commonly used than the ones listed here.

The Measure-Object cmdlet

The **Measure-Object** cmdlet has a simple function. It calculates statistics based on the objects in the pipeline. Its most basic form takes no parameters, and simply counts the objects that are in the pipeline.

To count the files in `c:\temp` and its subfolders, you could write:

```
Dir c:\temp -recurse -file | Measure-Object
```

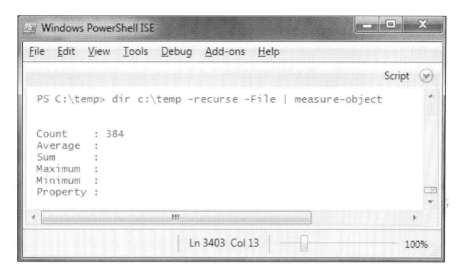

The output shows the count, and also some other properties that give a hint about the other uses of the cmdlet. To populate these other fields, you will need to provide the name of the property that is used to calculate them and also specify which field(s) you want to calculate. The calculations are specified using the `-Sum`, `-Minimum`, `-Maximum`, and `-Average` switches.

For instance, to add up (sum) the lengths of the files in the `C:\Windows` directory, you could issue this command:

```
Dir c:\Windows | Measure-Object -Property Length -Sum
```

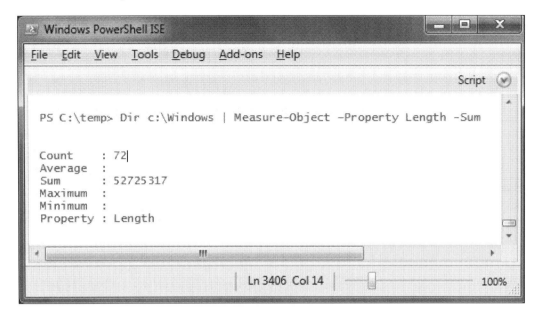

 You try it!

Use the `Measure-Object` cmdlet to find the size of the largest file on your `C:`.

The Group-Object cmdlet

The **Group-Object** cmdlet divides the objects in the pipeline into distinct sets based on a property or a set of properties. For instance, we can categorize the files in a folder by their extensions using Group-Object like this:

```
Administrator: Windows PowerShell                                              _ □ X
PS C:\temp> dir c:\temp | Group-Object -property Extension

Count Name                  Group
----- ----                  -----
    4                       {files, PowerShellCookbook, WORDsearch, test}
    2 .zip                  {2-ef5-m2-dbfirst-exercise-files.zip, Chapter1_1stDraft.zip}
    1 .publishsettings      {3-Month Free Trial-6-17-2013-credentials.publishsettings}
    7 .txt                  {abcde.txt, computers.txt, ErrorServers.txt, newfile.txt...}
   18 .ps1                  {adv_event1.ps1, datefolder.ps1, get-extension.ps1, get-powershellversionmessage.ps1...
    1 .psm1                 {AreaFunctions.psm1}
    3 .html                 {blogs.html, localhost.html, test.html}
    2 .opml                 {blogs.opml, blogs2.opml}
    2 .xml                  {books.xml, file.xml}
    1 .log                  {cbs.log}
    1 .ps1xml               {chapt4_ping_status.ps1xml}
    4 .jpg                  {driversLicense.jpg, gwen_birth.jpg, marriage.jpg, release.jpg}
    3 .csv                  {FileList.csv, issues.csv, ServerList.csv}
    1 .cmd                  {install.cmd}
    1 .docx                 {Manuscript Questionnaire 1P - RavenDB in Action.docx}
    1 .cer                  {MikeAzure.cer}
    5 .xps                  {ricepudding.xps, roses.xps, wallflowers.xps, werthers.xps...}
    1 .sql                  {sampledatabase.sql}
    1 .clixml               {SQL.clixml}
    2 .dll                  {System.Management.Automation.dll, System.Management.Automation.Resources.dll}
    2 .FDB                  {TESTADO (2).FDB, TESTADO.FDB}
    1 .psd1                 {testmanifest.psd1}
    1 .exe                  {VisualStudioHelpDownloader2012.exe}
    1 .config               {VisualStudioHelpDownloader2012.exe.config}
    1 .chm                  {WindowsPowerShell2.0CoreHelp-May2011.chm}

PS C:\temp>
```

You will notice in the output that PowerShell has provided the count of items in each set, the value of the property (Extension) that labels the set, and a property called **Group**, which contains all of the original objects that were on the pipeline that ended up in the set. If you have used the GROUP BY clause in SQL and are used to losing the original information when you group, you'll be pleased to know that PowerShell retains those objects in their original state in the Group property of the output.

You try it!

Can you think of a way to get the original objects out of the Group property? (Hint: one of the ways to use Select-Object might come in handy here.)

If you don't need the objects and are simply concerned with what the counts are, you can use the -NoElement switch, which causes the Group property to be omitted.

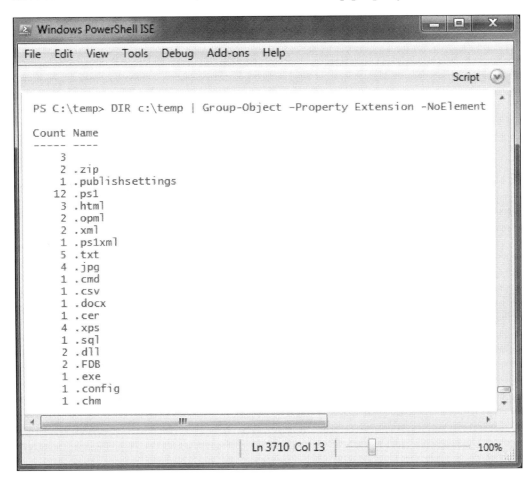

You're not limited to grouping by a single property either. If you want to see files grouped by mode (read-only, archive, etc.) and extension, you can simply list both properties.

```
Windows PowerShell ISE

File   Edit   View   Tools   Debug   Add-ons   Help

                                                      Script

PS C:\temp> dir | group-object Mode,Extension -NoElement

Count Name
----- ----
    2 d----,
    2 -a---, .zip
    1 -a---, .publishsettings
   12 -a---, .ps1
    3 -a---, .html
    2 -a---, .opml
    2 -a---, .xml
    1 -a---, .ps1xml
    4 -a---, .txt
    4 -a---, .jpg
    1 -----, .cmd
    1 -a---, .csv
    1 -a---, .docx
    1 -a---, .cer
    1 -ar--, .xps
    3 -a---, .xps
    1 -a---, .sql
    2 -a---, .dll
    1 -a---,
    2 -a---, .FDB
    1 -a---, .exe
    1 -a---, .config
    1 -a---, .chm

                  Ln 4387 Col 13                         100%
```

Note that the Name property of each set is now a list of two values corresponding to the two properties defining the group.

The Group-Object cmdlet can be useful to summarize the objects, but you will probably not use it nearly as much as Sort-Object, Where-Object, and Select-Object.

Putting them together

The several *-Object cmdlets that we've discussed in this chapter will be the foundation to your experience with PowerShell. Although, we only used them with Dir, Get-Service, and Get-Process, this is only because I can be sure that you can use these cmdlets on any system. The way that you use the *-Object cmdlets is the same whether you're dealing with files and folders, virtual machines, or mailboxes in Exchange. Since PowerShell gives you objects in all of these situations, these cmdlets will enable you to manipulate them using the same techniques.

Here are a couple of concrete examples of how the methods of using these cmdlets are portable between the types of objects. First, to get the largest five files in the c:\Windows folder, you would do this:

```
Dir c:\Windows | Sort-Object -Property Length -Descending |
Select-Object -First 5
```

Similarly, getting the five processes that are using the most file handles would look like this:

```
Get-Process | Sort-Object -Property Handles -Descending |
Select-Object -First 5
```

Can you see that the methodology to solve these two problems is exactly the same? Can you think of other problems that you might solve using a similar approach?

You Try it!
Use the cmdlets in this chapter to find the five newest files on your C: drive (use the LastWriteTime property to determine the age).

Summary

In this chapter, we looked at how to use the pipeline in PowerShell and several of the cmdlets that deal with objects in general. Once you learn to use these cmdlets efficiently, you will be able to solve all kinds of interesting problems in many areas.

In the next chapter, we will investigate PowerShell's versatile formatting system and learn how to format output in different ways.

For further reading

- Get-Help about_pipelines
- Get-Help Sort-Object
- Get-Help Where-Object
- Get-Help Select-Object
- Get-Help Group-Object
- Get-Help about_comparison_operators
- Get-Help about_scriptblocks

5
Formatting Output

So far, we are aware of PowerShell formatting the output of the commands that we execute, but we haven't spent any time on the particular ways that the output is formatted. That changes in this chapter. Now, we will learn all about the PowerShell formatting system and how we can take advantage of it. The topics covered in this chapter include the following:

- When does formatting occur?
- The rules of automatic formatting
- The cmdlets that control formatting
- The dangers of formatting
- The best practices of formatting

When does formatting occur?

The first thing to understand about PowerShell formatting is that the host you are in always formats the output. Remember that the host is the application (for example, the PowerShell console or the ISE) that is running the PowerShell engine and executing the commands that you enter. Since we know that cmdlets always output objects, the presence of some kind of formatting system is clear when we look at the output of a cmdlet such as `dir` (or `Get-ChildItem`):

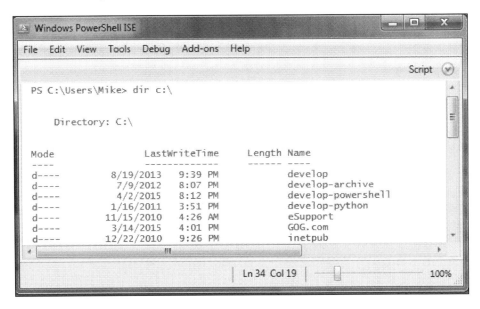

Somehow, certain properties are displayed and others are hidden. In this output, we can even see that the objects are grouped by a particular property (`PSParentPath`) by the display of **Directory: C:** at the top.

When the host executes a pipeline (and any line of code is a pipeline), it appends the `Out-Default` cmdlet to the end of the pipeline. The `Out-Default` cmdlet's job is to send the objects to the default formatter. The default formatter follows a set of rules to convert the output objects into special formatting objects. The host knows how to output the formatting objects, so you can see the formatted data. The trick to formatting in PowerShell is to know the rules.

Note

If you go down the advanced route and write your own host application, you have a control over whether `Out-Default` is called. For instance, if you wanted to display output in a grid rather than in text, you wouldn't want the formatting system to get in the way and format the objects for you.

The rules of automatic formatting

PowerShell formatting is somewhat complex and can be confusing at first. In fact, there are only a few basic rules:

- Format files specify the formatting for specific types
- Formatting decisions are based on the first object in the pipeline
- Objects with four or less properties are formatted as tables
- Objects with five or more properties are formatted as lists

Formatting files

In `$PSHOME`, there are files whose names end with `format.ps1xml`. These files are XML files that specify the default formatting specifications for many of the types of objects that you will work with in PowerShell. These files are loaded by the host when the PowerShell session starts. If you write your own format files, you can load them using the `Update-FormatData` cmdlet. The details of writing your own format files are beyond the scope of this book, but a quick read through the `FileSystem.Format.ps1xml` file will make some things clear:

```
FileSystem.format.ps1xml  X
 17  <Configuration>
 18      <SelectionSets>
 19          <SelectionSet>
 20              <Name>FileSystemTypes</Name>
 21              <Types>
 22                  <TypeName>System.IO.DirectoryInfo</TypeName>
 23                  <TypeName>System.IO.FileInfo</TypeName>
 24              </Types>
 25          </SelectionSet>
 26      </SelectionSets>
 27
 28      <!-- ############### GLOBAL CONTROL DEFINITIONS ############### -->
 29      <Controls>
 30          <Control>
 31              <Name>FileSystemTypes-GroupingFormat</Name>
 32                  <CustomControl>
 33                      <CustomEntries>
 34                          <CustomEntry>
 35                              <CustomItem>
 36                                  <Frame>
```

In this file, first, we can see that the formatting is selected by the objects of the `System.IO.DirectoryInfo` and `System.IO.FileInfo` types. Second, the first view specified is grouped by `PSParentPath` and we can see the properties listed (`Mode`, `LastWriteTime`, `Length`, and `Name`) in the table format. These two observations match what we see, when we execute the `Get-ChildItem` cmdlet against a file system path.

Formatting decisions are based on the first object

Knowing that the type of objects are matched against the formatting specified in the files is part of the equation. The next thing to know is that PowerShell relies on the first object in the pipeline to determine what formatting to apply. If subsequent objects don't "fit" in that format, PowerShell will revert to a list display, listing the property names and values separated by a colon. To illustrate this, we can join two different pipelines together using a semicolon. This will cause the output of both pipelines to be treated as if they were from the same pipeline. The first part of the pipeline is outputting the first item in the root of C: and the second is outputting the first process:

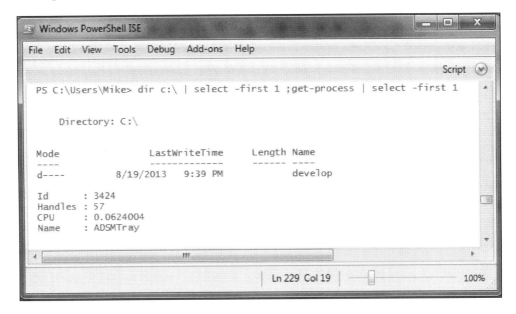

The pipeline we executed outputted a single `DirectoryInfo` object as well as a `process` object. PowerShell selected the default, tabular view for the `DirectoryInfo` object, but the Process object doesn't fit in this format. Thus, the Process object was formatted in a generic way, listing the properties one per line.

If we reverse the pipeline, we'll see that the Process object gets its specified format and the `DirectoryInfo` object is generically treated:

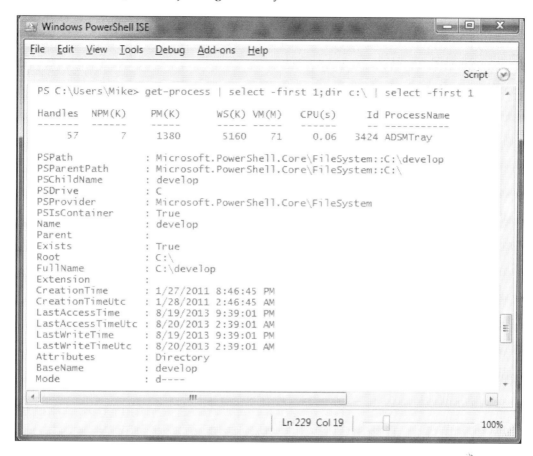

Another thing that can be confusing is that if we use `Select-Object` to limit the properties output, the resulting object is no longer of the original type. For example, we execute the following:

```
Dir | Select-Object –Property Name,Length
```

Here, we would no longer be outputting the `System.IO.FileInfo` and `System.IO.DirectoryInfo` objects, but the `Selected.System.IO.FileInfo` and `Selected.System.IO.DirectoryInfo` objects. These new objects would not be selected by the same format files, because the type is different.

Small objects go in a table

If the objects being formatted don't match a format file, one of the rules of formatting says that small objects with four or less properties are formatted as a table. We can verify this using `Select-Object` as mentioned in the last section to create new objects that don't match the existing format file:

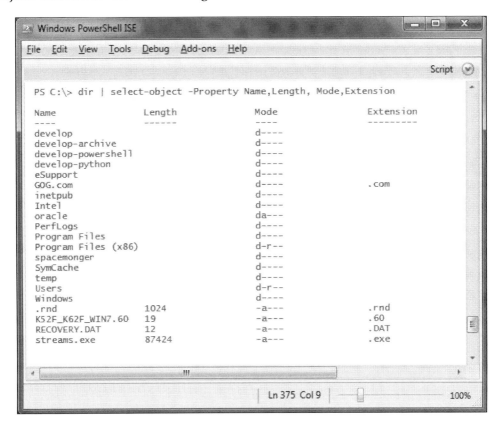

As expected, not only do we avoid the grouped format that we saw before for `Dir` output, but we also got the data in a table since there were only four properties.

Sometimes, we find that the table format that is generated doesn't look very nice. The engine divides the line evenly into the number of columns that are required. It also formats each column according to the type of data in the properties of the first object, left-aligning strings and right-aligning numbers. Look at the output of the two commands in the following screenshot, and you will see that the spacing of both of the tables is looking somewhat ridiculous. We'll see later in the chapter what we can do to improve this situation, but for now, we just need to be aware that sometimes default formatting is less than perfect:

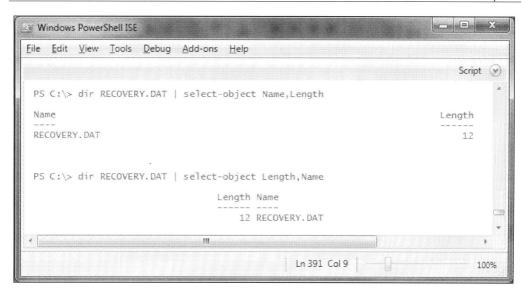

Another issue with formatting in a table is that sometimes the properties don't fit very well in the columns. When this happens, PowerShell will truncate the value and end the display with an ellipsis (. . .):

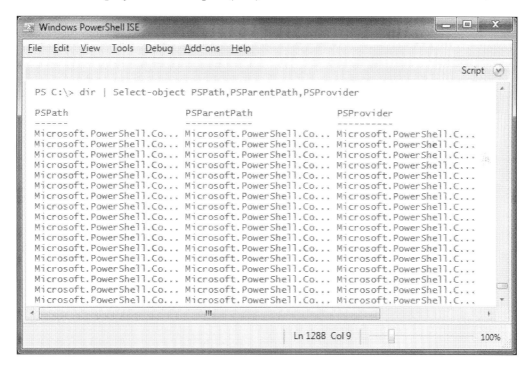

Large objects go in a list

Objects that are larger than four properties are placed into what PowerShell calls a list format, placing each property of each object in a separate line, and separating the property name from the property value with a colon. We saw this format earlier when an object did not fit in the format selected by the first object in the pipeline.

Continuing the examples using `Dir`, we can see this format in action. Adding a fifth property to the `Select-Object` cmdlet causes the output to be formatted as a list:

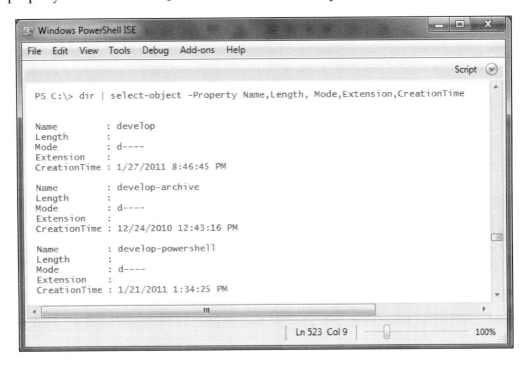

List formats can seem cleaner than tabular formats because there is less room for issues with column widths and left and right justification. On the other hand, the output is spread over a lot more lines and is harder to scan visually.

> Since default formats can cause properties to be omitted from the output, it is often convenient to use `Select-Object` to create new "Selected" objects that skip these formats. To see all the properties, you can use a wildcard (such as *) to match everything.
>
> Try this, for example: `Dir | Select-Object –Property *`

Cmdlets that control formatting

The rules in the previous section covered all the output where we haven't specifically told PowerShell how to format. What is nice here is that the default formats for many of the types that are commonly encountered in PowerShell do a good job of displaying the most often used properties, and the rules to format other objects are also, generally, very appropriate. But in some circumstances, we want to have more control over the output, and it's no surprise that PowerShell provides cmdlets for this purpose.

Format-Table and Format-List

The two most commonly used formatting cmdlets are `Format-Table` and `Format-List`. As their names suggest, they force the formatting system to use either a table or a list format for the objects, irrespective of the number of properties or the type-related formatting files that might be present. Each of the cmdlets has a `-Property` parameter that takes a list of properties to be included. A couple of quick examples should make the basic usage clear.

First, we can use `Format-List` with the long property value example we saw earlier, which led to an unusable table, to see how this would look like as a list:

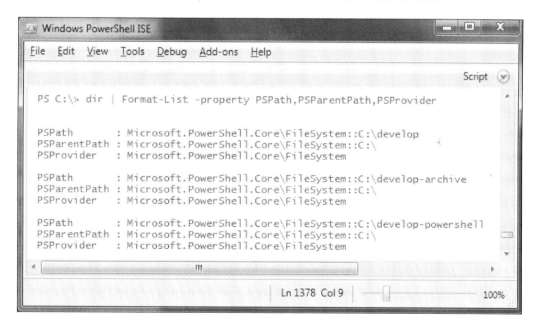

Clearly, the output makes a lot more sense as a list.

Also, we can use `Format-Table` to output a series of objects that would, normally, have been formatted as a list because they have more than four properties. Since we know the properties in this case are numeric, formatting as a table is reasonable:

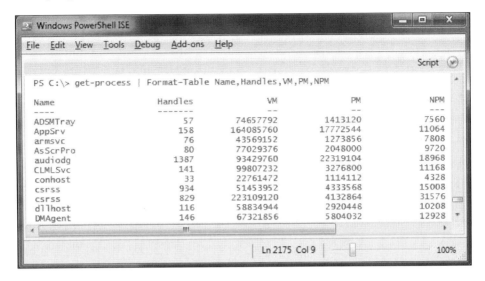

In this case, we still have some open spaces, so we can utilize the `-AutoSize` switch parameter to improve the output format even more. `AutoSize` tells the formatting system to look at all the values in all the columns before deciding on the column sizes (instead of dividing the line evenly):

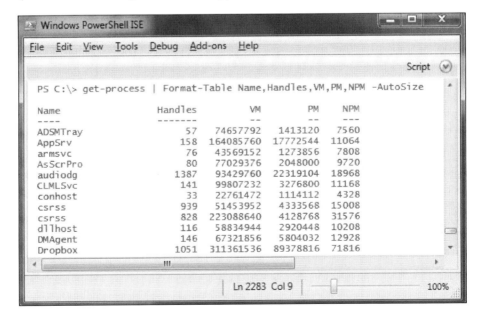

If the number of objects is not very high, using `AutoSize` can make the tables much nicer to look at. The `-AutoSize` switch will also help the awkward looking tables, which we saw with two columns, either at the margins or crowded at the center of the page:

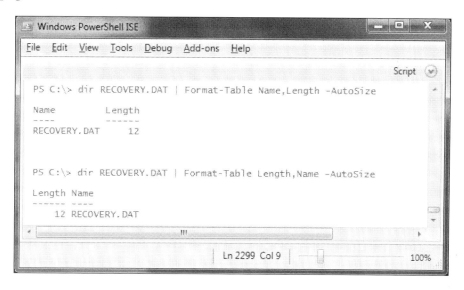

The dangers of formatting

The automatic formatting of objects makes the PowerShell experience much more comfortable. Seeing familiar looking output and commonly used properties is a great aid to productivity. However, formatting comes with a price. Simply put, formatted objects are not able to be used like the original objects were. For instance, once objects are formatted, there is no way to sort or filter them based on properties. Formatting can be compared with taking pictures of the objects. The picture looks similar to the objects, but are not the actual objects. The only thing that can be done with the formatted objects is to output them somewhere. As mentioned earlier, the `Out-Default` cmdlet sends them to the console. Additionally, the `Out-File`, `Out-Printer`, and `Out-String` cmdlets send the output (obviously) to a file, printer, and string.

Attempting to use the formatted objects in the same way that we've grown accustomed to using objects, fails miserably, as seen from the following screenshot:

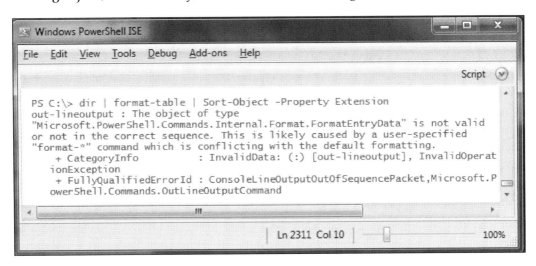

Best practices of formatting

Since formatting objects leads to objects that can no longer be manipulated, it is a best practice to avoid formatting anything that you want to be able to manipulate. This seems obvious, but it is easy to get wrong. We will talk about this best practice at length in the chapters covering Scripts and Functions.

Summary

In this chapter, we have walked through the PowerShell formatting system. We saw that PowerShell hosts use Out-Default to cause formatting to happen to all the output. We looked at the rules to format objects, when no explicit formatting instructions are included, as well as the cmdlets to tell PowerShell exactly how we want objects to be formatted. Finally, we discovered that formatting is something of a destructive operation, in which the original objects are no longer available after the formatting has occurred.

In the next chapter, we will take our first steps towards packaging sequences of commands for reuse in scripts.

For further reading

- `Get-Help about_format.ps1xml`
- `Get-Help Out-Default`
- `Get-Help Format-Table`
- `Get-Help Format-List`
- `Get-Help Update-FormatData`

6
Scripts

Now that we have learned some useful commands, it would be nice to be able to record a sequence of commands, so that we can execute them all at once. In this chapter, we will learn how to accomplish this with scripts. We will also cover the following topics:

- Execution policies
- Adding parameters to scripts
- Control structures
- Profiles

Packaging commands

Saving commands in a file for reuse is a pretty simple idea. In PowerShell, the simplest kind of these files is called a script and it uses the `.ps1` extension, no matter what version of PowerShell you're using. For example, if you wanted to create a new folder, under `c:\temp`, with the current date as the name and then change to that folder, you could put these commands in a file:

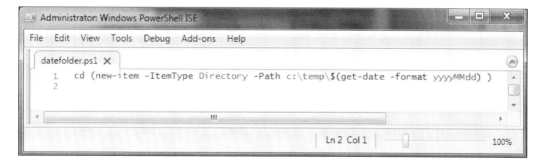

Note that I'm using the top portion of the ISE to edit the file contents and I have saved the file as dateFolder.ps1 in the c:\temp folder. To run the script, you can simply type the name of the file at prompt as follows (in the bottom portion of the ISE):

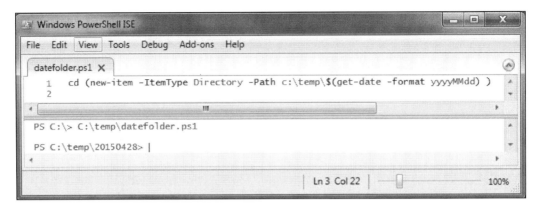

If you have the file loaded in the ISE, you can also use the **Run** button on the toolbar to run the current file.

It's possible that when you try to run this script, you will receive an error complaining about the execution policy, instead of seeing the current path being set to a new folder. To understand why this would have happened, we need to discuss the concept of execution policies.

Execution policy

Execution policy is a safety feature in PowerShell that enables the system to control which scripts are able to be run. I say *safety* instead of *security* because execution policy is trivial to circumvent. Execution policy are more like the safety of a gun, which prevents accidental discharge of the weapon. An execution policy is an attempt to prevent users from accidentally executing scripts.

Possible execution policy values include the following:

- Restricted
- AllSigned
- RemoteSigned
- Unrestricted

The Restricted setting means that the scripts cannot be run at all. AllSigned means that all scripts must be digitally signed to run. Unrestricted says that any script will run. RemoteSigned is a middle-ground setting that says that any local scripts will run, but scripts from remote sources (like the Internet or untrusted UNC paths) need to be digitally signed.

Prior to Windows Server 2012R2, the default execution policy for all systems was Restricted, meaning that by default scripts were not allowed to run at all. With Server 2012R2, the default was changed to RemoteSigned.

Attempting to run a script when the execution policy does not permit it, results in an error such as the following:

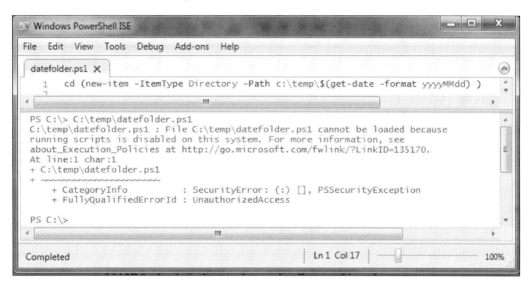

To see what your current execution policy is set to, use the Get-ExecutionPolicy cmdlet. To set the execution policy, you would use the Set-ExecutionPolicy cmdlet.

Important!
Since the execution policy is a system setting, changing it requires you to run an elevated session. Attempting to change the execution policy from a user session, will result in an "Access Denied" error writing to the registry.

The following figure shows the results of running the script after the execution policy has been set to an appropriate level:

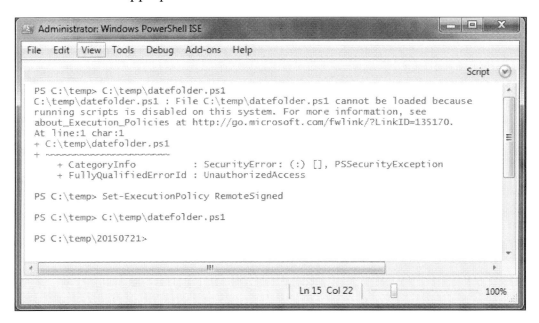

In my experience, the `RemoteSigned` setting is most practical. However, in a secure environment such as a production data center, I can easily see that using an `AllSigned` policy could make sense.

Types of scripts

The PowerShell community often distinguishes between two different kinds of scripts. Some scripts, called **controller scripts**, call other cmdlets, scripts, and functions to complete a process. Controller scripts sometimes do more than one thing, but they are not meant for reuse, except perhaps as a step in a larger controller script. You might expect to find a controller script scheduled to run in the task scheduler. **Tool scripts**, on the other hand, are more focused, perform a single action, and are intended specifically to be reused. A tool script would never run on its own, let alone be scheduled. There aren't any technical differences between the two kinds of scripts, but there are things that would be considered best practices for one type that wouldn't be appropriate for the other. I find the distinction between the tools and controllers useful. When you write a script, think about whether it is a standalone process (controller), or it is something that you will use as a component in solving problems (tool).

Scopes and scripts

When you run a script, the PowerShell engine creates what is called a **scope** for the execution. If your script creates or modifies variables or functions (which we will discuss in later chapters), these changes will be created in the script's scope and will be removed at the end of the execution of the script. In the next chapter on PowerShell functions, we will see an important consequence of this, but for now we should just know that the things that are done in the script don't leave the script. As an example, here is a script that sets a variable to my name and outputs the variable to verify that it was correctly set. After executing the script, checking the variable shows that it is no longer set:

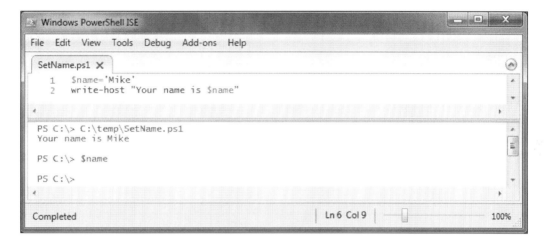

If we need the things in the script to remain after its execution, PowerShell provides the ability to **dot-source** the file rather than just executing it. Dot-sourcing means to execute something, but to do it in the current scope and not create a child scope for it. The effect of dot-sourcing a script is the same as executing the commands in the script at the command-line—that is, all the effects of the script remain. To dot-source something, you use a period (a dot) and then a space, and then the name of the script.

If we dot-source the script from the previous example (instead of simply executing it), we can see that the $name variable retains the value that was set in the script:

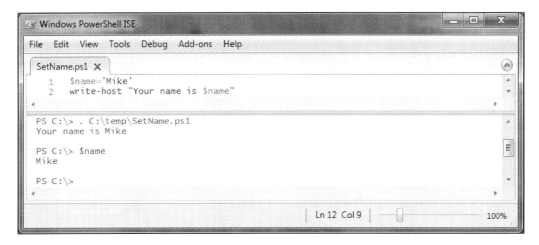

Parameters add flexibility

Executing a series of commands can be useful, but often you will want to execute the scripts and also provide some input—specific details about the execution of the script. One way to do this is to use **parameters**. Parameters are a way for you to provide the values that you want to be used in a script at execution time. For example, you might find that when you create a new directory, you immediately want to change to that directory. We started the chapter with a similar script that created a folder named with the current date, but because the script determined the folder name, we didn't need to provide any input. For this script, we don't know when we write the script what the name of the folder should be, but we will when we run it.

Parameters for scripts are specified in a `Param()` statement at the beginning of the script. The names of the parameters are variables and start with a dollar sign (`$`). You aren't limited to a single parameter, either. You can include multiple parameters, separating them with commas. We will spend a lot more time talking about parameters when we talk about functions, but the following screenshot should illustrate how to use parameters in scripts:

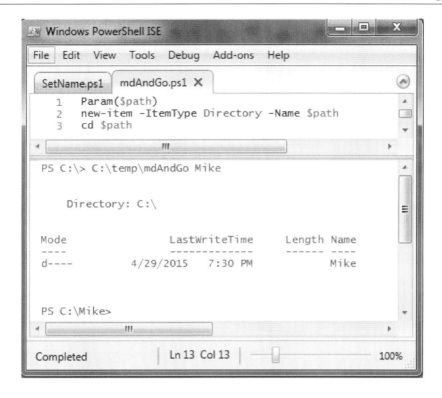

Adding some logic

PowerShell would not be very useful if scripts were limited to running one command after another without any logic. As expected from a modern language, PowerShell includes a full complement of control structures to allow you to vary the execution in just about any way you'd like. We will briefly introduce the most common control structures.

Conditional logic (IF)

The most simple logic statement is the `If` statement. The `If` statement allows you to have some code executed, if and only if a particular condition is met. In its simplest form, the `If` statement includes a condition in parentheses and a scriptblock to be executed when the condition is true:

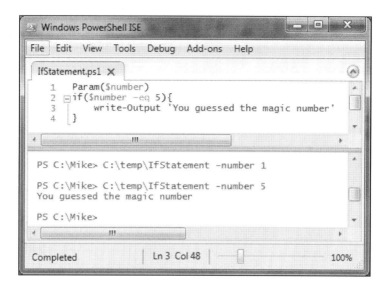

If there is another condition that should be executed if the first condition is false, you can include an `Else` clause:

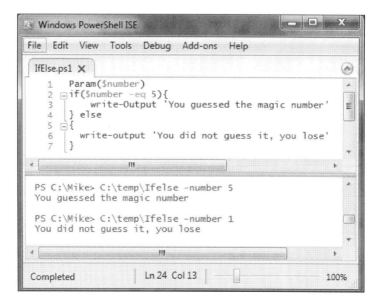

If you have multiple conditions to test, there is an ElseIf clause as well. Here's an example of its use:

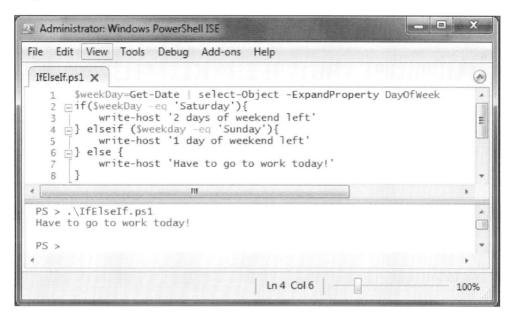

Looping logic

The most common way to loop in PowerShell is the ForEach statement. ForEach causes a scriptblock to be executed for each item in a collection. The ForEach statement lets you name the placeholder that is used to refer to the individual items in the collection. The syntax for the ForEach statement looks as follows:

```
ForEach ($placeholder in $collection){
  #Code goes here
}
```

As an example, we can display the extensions of all of the files in a folder using ForEach:

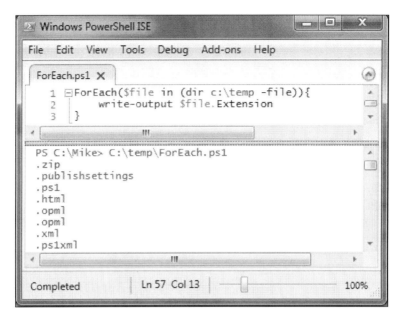

If you remember from *Chapter 4, Life on the Assembly Line* there is also a ForEach-Object cmdlet that works in a pipeline and executes a scriptblock for each item in the pipeline. To make things even more confusing, ForEach-Object has an alias called ForEach. It's easy to get confused between the ForEach statement and the ForEach-Object cmdlet, but remember that the ForEach statement does not work in a pipeline and lets you name the placeholder, so if it's in a pipeline, it has to be the ForEach-Object cmdlet.

More logic

There are other statements that can be used to structure scripts, but If and ForEach are by far the most common. If you need to use others, they are well documented in PowerShell's awesome help content.

For quick reference, some of the other statements include the following:

Statement	Purpose
`While`	Executes a scriptblock as long as a condition is true
`Do..Until`	Executes a scriptblock until a condition is true
`For`	Executes a scriptblock for each number in a range (like 1 to 10)

Profiles

Profiles are special scripts that PowerShell hosts run automatically when they start a new session. Each host looks in four different locations for profile scripts, running any of them that it finds. To find where these locations are, for the host you're in, look at the `$profile` automatic variable:

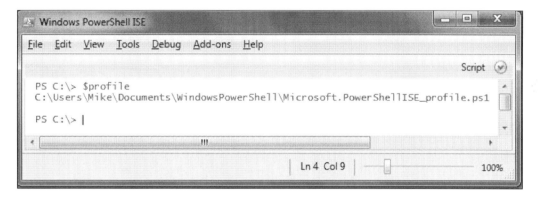

The first thing you'll notice is that there's only one path listed. To see all of them, you have to look at the extra properties that have been spliced onto `$profile`:

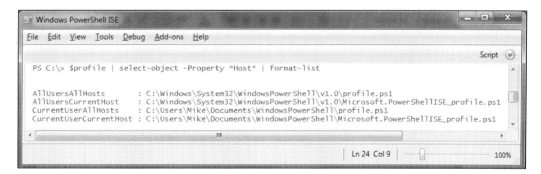

The names of these properties should give you a good idea when each of them is used. The `AllHosts` profiles are used by all the hosts. The `AllUsers` profiles are used by all the users. The `CurrentHost` profiles are used by the host you're in (console or ISE). The `CurrentUser` profiles are specific to the user running this PowerShell session. It might be helpful to see the output of the same command from the PowerShell console instead of the ISE. The `AllHosts` profiles are the same, but the `CurrentHost` profiles are different, specific to that host.

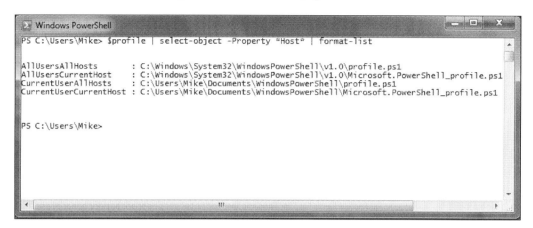

You can put any code you want in your profile. At this point in the book, we don't have a lot of things that would be useful, but we could at least change the directory to a more useful location than `$PSHome`. Since profiles are scripts, they are subject to the execution policy limitations. This means if your execution policy is still set to `Restricted`, the host won't be able to run your profile script, even if it is in the right place. Similarly, if your execution policy is `AllSigned`, you would need to digitally sign your profile scripts.

Summary

Scripts offer a useful way to combine commands and reuse them later. In this chapter, we saw how to create and execute scripts. We learned about using parameters to make scripts more flexible and how to incorporate logic into a script using a few control structures.

In the next chapter, we will look at another way to package code for reuse: namely, functions.

For further reading

- Get-Help about_scripts
- Get-Help about_execution_policies
- Get-Help Set-ExecutionPolicy
- Get-Help about_scopes
- Get-Help about_parameters
- Get-Help about_profiles
- Get-Help about_if
- Get-Help about_foreach
- Get-Help about_switch
- Get-Help about_do
- Get-Help about_while
- Get-Help about_switch
- Get-Help about_for
- Get-Help about_break
- Get-Help about_continue

7
Functions

In the previous chapter, we learned about packaging a set of commands in a script. In this chapter, we will look at using functions to provide the same kind of containment. We will discuss the differences between functions and scripts, and drill down more into parameters. The specific topics covered in this chapter include the following:

- Defining functions
- Comparing scripts and functions
- Executing functions
- Comment-based help
- Function output
- Parameters
- Default values

Another kind of container

Scripts are a simple way to reuse your commands. Scripts are file-based, so there is an inherent limitation—you can only have one script per file. This may not seem like a problem, but when you have hundreds or even thousands of pieces of code, you may want to be able to group them together and not have so many files on the disk.

Comparing scripts and functions

The primary difference between a function and a script is that a script is a file, whereas a function is contained within a file. Consider the MdAndGo.ps1 script from *Chapter 6, Scripts*:

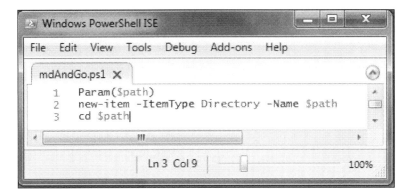

As a function, this could be written like this:

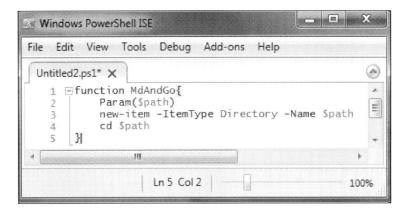

You can see from this example that the functions are defined using the function keyword. Comparing these two examples, you can also see that the body of the function (the scriptblock after the function name) is identical to the contents of the script. Practically speaking, anything you can do in a script, you can do in a function also. If this is true (it is true), why would we want to use functions?

The first reason is simple convenience. If I write a dozen bits of code pertaining to a particular subject area, I would want these bits of code to be in one place. If I use scripts, I can put all of these in the same folder, and this gives a bit of coherence. On the other hand, if I use functions, I can put all of these functions in the same file. Since they're all in the same file, I can edit the file all at once and make the changes to the functions more easily. Seeing the functions in the same file can help to understand the relationships between the code, and into repeated code or possibilities for refactoring.

Second, functions are exposed in PowerShell via a PSDrive called Function:. I can see all of the functions that have been loaded into my current session using cmdlets such as Get-ChildItem, or its commonly used alias dir:

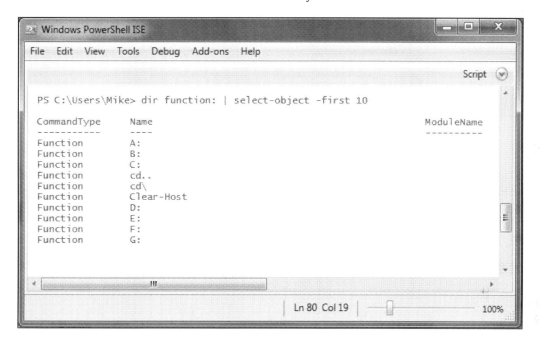

PSProviders and PSDrives

PowerShell uses PSProviders and PSDrives to provide access to hierarchical data sources using the same cmdlets that you would use to access filesystems. The Function: drive, mentioned here, holds all the functions loaded into the current session. Other PSDrives include the registry drives (HKLM: and HCKU:), the Variable: drive, the ENV: drive of environment variables, and the Cert: drive that provides access to the certificate store.

Executing and calling functions

As seen in figure in the *Comparing scripts and functions* section, defining a function involves using the `function` keyword and surrounding the code you want with a scriptblock. Executing this function statement simply adds the function definition to the current PowerShell session. To subsequently call the function, you use the function name like you would a cmdlet name, and supply parameters and arguments just like you would for a cmdlet or script.

Storing the `MdAndGo` function in a file called `MdAndGo.ps1` can be confusing because we're using the same name for the two things. You dot-source the `ps1` file to load the function into the session, then you can execute this function. Dot-sourcing the file doesn't run the function. If we had written this as a script, on the other hand, we could have executed the logic of the script without dot-sourcing.

Warning!

A common mistake of new PowerShell users is to call a function using parentheses to surround the parameters and commas to separate them. When you do this, PowerShell thinks you are creating an array and passes the array as an argument to the first parameter.

Naming conventions

Looking at the list of functions in the Function: drive, you will see some odd ones, such as CD.., CD\, and A:. These are created to help the command-line experience and are not typical functions. The names of these functions, though, show an interesting difference between functions and scripts, since it should be clear that you can't have a file named A:.ps1. Function naming, in general, should follow the same naming convention as cmdlets, namely Verb-Noun, where the verb is from the verb list returned by Get-Verb and the noun is a singular noun that consistently identifies what kinds of things are being referred to. Our MdAndGo function, for example, should have been named according to this standard. One reasonable name would be Set-NewFolderLocation.

Comment-based help

Simply defining a function creates a very basic help entry. Here's the default help for the MdAndGo function that we wrote earlier in the chapter:

We haven't given PowerShell enough to build a useful help entry, but fortunately for us there is a simple way to include help content through comments. This feature in PowerShell is called comment-based help and is documented thoroughly in the about_comment_based_help help topic. For our purposes, we will add enough information to show that we're able to affect the help output, but we won't go into much detail.

With comment-based help, you will include a specially formatted comment immediately before the function. Keywords in the comment indicate where the help system should get the text for different areas in the help topic. Here's what our function looks like with an appropriate comment:

```
1  <#
2  .Synopsis
3      Creates a folder and sets the location to it
4  .DESCRIPTION
5      This function takes the path of a folder to create as a parameter,
6      creates it and then sets the location to the new folder.
7  .EXAMPLE
8      MdAndGo c:\temp\test1
9  .EXAMPLE
10     MdAndGo E:\example2
11 .INPUTS
12     Does not accept pipeline input
13 .OUTPUTS
14     Outputs the folder that was created
15
16 #>
17 function MdAndGo{
18     Param($path)
19     new-item -ItemType Directory -Name $path
20     cd $path
21 }
22
```

After executing the file to create the function, we can test the comment-based help using get-help MdAndGo, just as before:

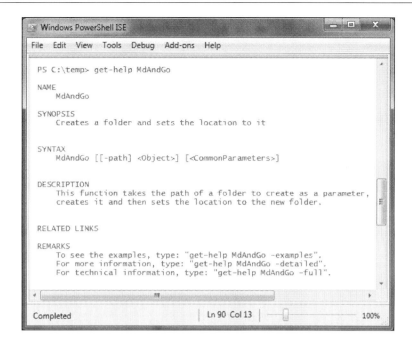

Since we included examples, we can either use the -Examples switch or use the really handy -ShowWindow switch:

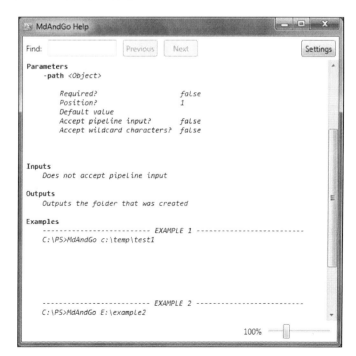

Note that we didn't need to number our examples or include the C:\PS> prompt. These are added automatically by the help system.

Parameters revisited

Just like scripts, functions can take parameters. Remember that parameters are placeholders, which let you vary the execution of the function (or script) based on the value that is passed to the parameter (called the argument). The MdAndGo function that we wrote earlier had a single parameter, but you can use as many parameters as you want. For instance, if you had a process that copied items from one folder to another and you wanted to write a function to make sure that both the source and destination folders already exist, you could write a function like this:

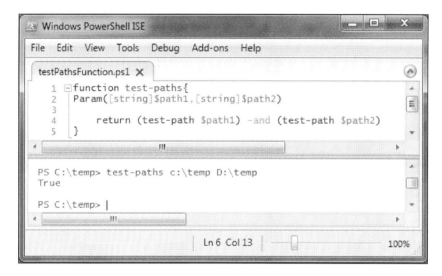

It should be clear from this example that parameters in the Param() statement are separated by commas. Remember that you don't use commas to separate the arguments you pass when you call the function. Also, the Param() statement needs to be the first statement in the function.

Typed parameters

Something else you might have noticed in this example is that we have specified that both the parameters have to be strings. It's hard to test this, since anything in the command-line is already a string. Let's write a function to output the average of two integers:

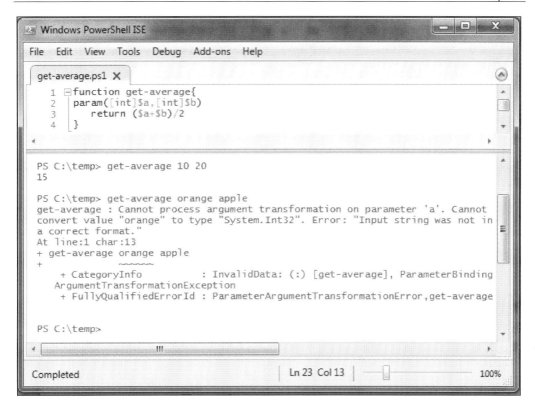

```
Windows PowerShell ISE

File  Edit  View  Tools  Debug  Add-ons  Help

get-average.ps1 X
  1 ⊟function get-average{
  2 │  param([int]$a,[int]$b)
  3 │     return ($a+$b)/2
  4 └}

PS C:\temp> get-average 10 20
15

PS C:\temp> get-average orange apple
get-average : Cannot process argument transformation on parameter 'a'. Cannot
convert value "orange" to type "System.Int32". Error: "Input string was not in
a correct format."
At line:1 char:13
+ get-average orange apple
+             ~~~~~~
    + CategoryInfo          : InvalidData: (:) [get-average], ParameterBinding
  ArgumentTransformationException
    + FullyQualifiedErrorId : ParameterArgumentTransformationError,get-average

PS C:\temp>

Completed                          Ln 23 Col 13                          100%
```

Here, we've used [int] to specify that the $a and $b parameters are integers. Specifying a type allows us to make certain assumptions about the values in these variables, namely, that they are numeric and it makes sense to average them. Other common types used in PowerShell are [String] and [DateTime].

The function works if you pass numeric arguments, but passing strings (such as orange and apple) causes an error. If you read the error message, you can see that PowerShell tried to figure out how to change "orange" into a number, but couldn't come up with a transformation that works. PowerShell has a very versatile parameter binding mechanism that attempts a number of methods to transform the arguments you pass into the type of parameters you have specified.

Switches

Besides using types like `string` and `int`, you can also use the **switch** type, which indicates a parameter that is either present or absent. We've seen switch parameters in cmdlets, such as the `-Recurse` switch parameter for `Get-ChildItem`. Remember that you don't specify an argument to a switch parameter. You either supply the parameter (such as `-Recurse`) or you don't. Switch parameters allow for easy on/off or true/false input. The parameter can be tested easily in an `if` statement like this:

Default values for parameters

You can also supply default values for parameters in the `Param()` statement. If no argument is given for a parameter that has a default, the default value is used for this parameter. Here's a simple example:

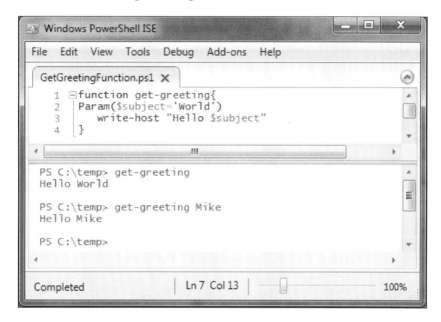

Using parameters is a powerful technique to make your functions applicable to more situations. This kind of flexibility is the key to write reusable functions.

Output

The functions that I've shown so far in this chapter have either explicitly used the return keyword, or used write-host to output text to the console instead of returning the data. However, the mechanism that PowerShell uses for function output is much more complex for several reasons.

The first complication is that the `return` keyword is completely optional. Consider the following four functions:

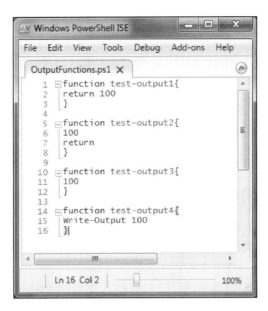

We can see that they all output the same value (`100`) by adding them all together:

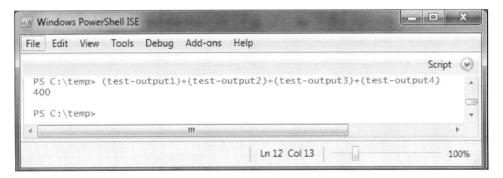

The reason that these functions do the same thing is that PowerShell uses the concept of streams to deal with data coming out of a function. Data that we consider "output" uses the output stream. Any value that isn't used somehow is written to the output stream, as is a value given in a return statement. A value can be used in many ways. Some common ways of using a value are:

- Assigning the value to a variable
- Using the value as a parameter to a function, script, or cmdlet

- Using the value in an expression
- Casting the value to [void] or piping it to Out-Null

 [void] is a special type that indicates that there is no actual value. Casting a value to [void] is essentially throwing away the value.

The last function, Test-Output4, shows that we can explicitly write to the output stream using write-output.

Another interesting feature of the output stream is that the values are placed in the output stream immediately, rather than waiting for the function to finish before outputting everything. If you consider running DIR C:\ -recurse, you can imagine that you would probably want to see the output before the whole process is complete, so this makes sense.

Functions are not limited to a single output value, either. As I stated earlier, *any value* that isn't used is output from the function. Thus, the following functions output two values and four values, respectively:

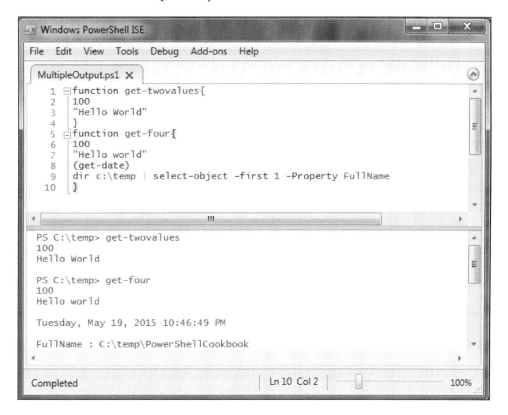

The output from these strange functions illustrates another property of PowerShell functions, namely, they can output more than one kind of object.

In practice, your functions will generally output one kind of object, but if you're not careful, you might accidentally forget to use a value somewhere and that value will become part of the output. This is a source of great confusion to PowerShell beginners, and can even cause people who have been using PowerShell to scratch their heads from time to time. The key is to be careful, and if in doubt, use `Get-Member` to see what kind of objects you get out of your function.

Summary

The functions in PowerShell are powerful and extremely useful to create flexible, reusable code. Parameters, including switch parameters, allow you to tailor the execution of a function to meet your needs. PowerShell functions behave differently from functions in many other languages, potentially outputting multiple objects of different types and at different times.

In the next chapter, we will look at PowerShell modules, a feature added in PowerShell 2.0 to help gather functions and scripts into libraries.

For further reading

- `Get-Help about_Functions`
- `Get-Help about_Parameters`
- `Get-Help about_Return`
- `Get-Help about_Comment_Based_Help`
- `Get-Help about_Providers`
- `Get-Help about_Core_Commands`

8
Modules

In the last two chapters, we learned about bundling code into scripts and functions. In this chapter, we will learn about using modules to bundle multiple functions or script files that are full of functions into a single container. There's more to modules than simply grouping things together. Altogether, we will learn the following:

- What is a module?
- Where do modules live?
- Loading and unloading a module
- PowerShell module autoloading

Packaging functions

We learned in the last two chapters that you can put a bunch of functions in a script file, and then dot-source this file to get these functions into a session. Consider the following script, called `AreaFunctions.ps1`:

After dot-sourcing the script file, we can use the functions and access the $pi variable as well. If we use get-command, we will find the functions but they are no longer connected in any way. That is, it is difficult to see that these functions are part of a unit. There is no data retained in the function definitions that tells us where they came from. Since one of the important points of PowerShell is that it is discoverable, this situation isn't ideal. PowerShell 2.0 introduced the concept of **modules** to help tie these functions (among other things) together.

Script modules

To turn this into a module in the simplest way, we can just change the file extension to .psm1. Once we have done this, we can import the module by pointing directly to the .psm1 file, as follows:

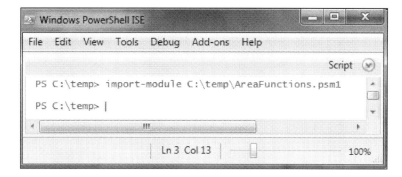

Similar to when we dot-sourced the script file, here we also don't see any real indication that the import-module cmdlet did anything. If we look at the output of get-command now, we can see that these functions are now listed as part of a module. We can, also, use the -Module parameter for get-command to show all the functions that were exported from the module:

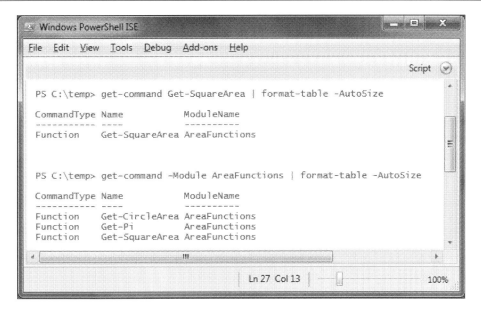

Now, these functions are much easier to discover, since we can see that they fit together somehow.

Module files with a `.psm1` extension are called script modules, for obvious reasons. One huge benefit of using script modules is that they are simple to create. Another reason for using script modules is that they provide the opportunity to hide elements that you don't want to be public.

In our module, the Get-Pi function is really just a helper function that is used to set the $pi variable (also, not super useful), which the Get-CircleArea function uses to perform its calculations. If we try to access $pi, we will find that the variable doesn't even exist. The reason is that by default, modules don't expose variables defined in them:

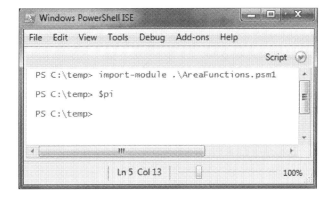

We'll see in the next section how to remedy this, but first, let's see how we can keep the Get-Pi function from being exposed as well.

The Export-ModuleMember cmdlet

The key to controlling which parts of a module are visible is to know the default visibility and how to use the Export-ModuleMember cmdlet.

By default, a module does the following:

- Exports all the functions
- Hides all the variables
- Hides all the aliases

If you don't like one of these, you can override it using the Export-ModuleMember cmdlet. This cmdlet has three parameters called -Function, -Variable, and -Alias, which let you list specifically which members (functions, variables, and aliases) you want to be exported. Since we are fine with the variable not being exported, and only want the two area functions exported, we can add this command at the end of the module to get the required configuration:

```
Export-ModuleMember -Function Get-SquareArea,Get-CircleArea
```

Warning!

If you include any Export-ModuleMember commands in your module, you need to specify all the members you want to export. For instance, if we wanted to export the Pi variable, we would have added the following:

```
Export-ModuleMember -variable Pi
```

If this was the only Export-ModuleMember command in the module, none of the functions would be exported. Also, note that we don't include $ when listing variable names in Export-ModuleMember.

Where do modules live?

PowerShell defines an environment variable called PSMODULEPATH, which contains a list of folders that it checks for modules. Viewing PSMODULEPATH is simplified by the -split operator to split the path wherever it sees a semicolon:

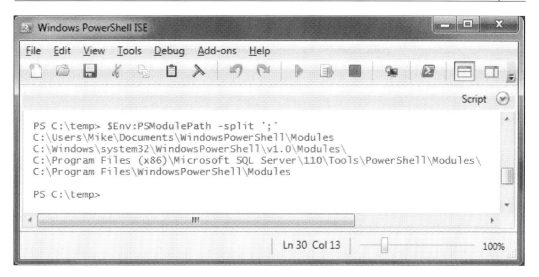

Here, you can see that there are four folders where PowerShell is looking for modules in this session. For it to find our AreaFunctions module, there needs to be a AreaFunctions subfolder in one of these locations with our psm1 file in it.

Once we have created a folder and placed the AreaFunctions.psm1 file in it, we can import the module by name rather than by path:

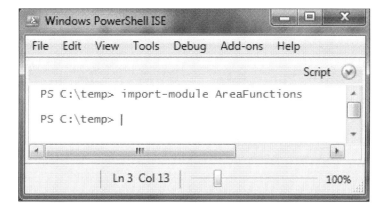

Removing a module

If you decide that you don't want the functions in a module included in your session for some reason, you can remove it using the `Remove-Module` cmdlet. Once the module is removed, you can try to check whether it was removed using the `Get-Command` cmdlet to look for one of the exported functions:

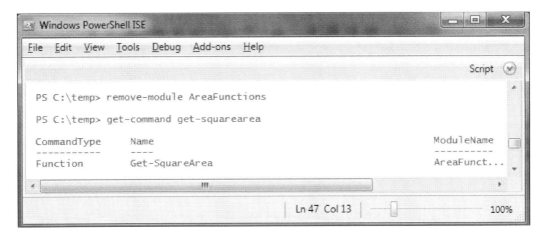

Wait a minute! We removed the module and it didn't give us an error, but then both the area functions are in the session and they have been reported as being in the `AreaFunctions` module. To understand what's going on, we need to understand module autoloading.

PowerShell module autoloading

In PowerShell 2.0 on Windows 2008 or Windows 7, there were only a handful of modules installed by the operating system, so knowing what modules were present and what commands were included in each module made sense. In PowerShell 3.0 with the CIM modules, the number of commands available jumped over 2,000, and it became unrealistic for users to be able to remember which of the scores of the modules contained in the commands were needed. To overcome this issue, PowerShell 3.0 introduced the concept of autoloading the modules. In PowerShell 3.0, if you reference a command that is not present in your session, PowerShell will look through the available modules (and in `PSMODULEPATH`), find the module that contains the missing command, and import it silently for you. This means that if your modules are installed in the correct directories, you don't have to use the `Import-Module` statements anymore.

When I first heard about module autoloading, I didn't like it. I thought I wanted to have a control over which modules were loaded and when they were loaded. I still use the `Import-Module` statements in scripts and modules to indicate dependencies, but I often rely on the autoloading behavior.

If you really don't want to use this feature, you can set the `$PSModuleAutoloadingPreference` variable to `None`. This will suppress the autoloading of modules, and force you to explicitly load modules using `Import-Module`.

The #Requires statement

Besides explicitly importing modules into a script, you can annotate the script with a special comment that tells the PowerShell engine that certain modules are required for the script to run. This is done using the `#Requires` statement. As `#Requires` starts with a number sign, it is a comment. However, this special comment has arguments like a cmdlet has. To indicate that a list of modules are required, simply list the module names, as shown in the following screenshot:

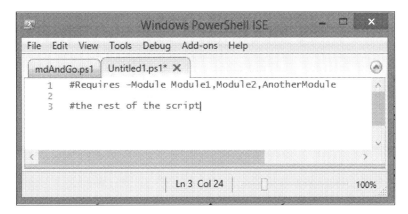

There are several other useful options possible with the `#Requires` statement. To see them, see the `about_Requires` help topic.

Removing a module – take two

We can adjust the $VerbosePreference, so that we can see what is going on behind the scenes when we remove and (silently) import a module:

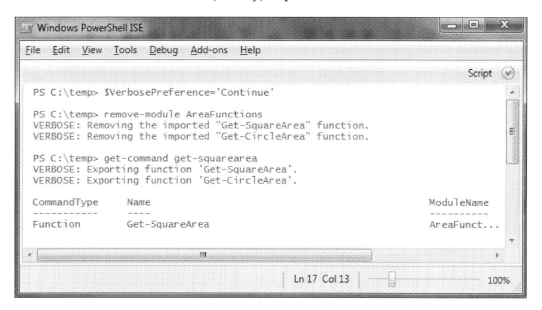

Manifest modules

While script modules are an improvement over dot-sourcing script files, manifest modules take modules to a new level entirely. A module manifest is a configuration file for a module that lets you provide information about the module and gives you control over what happens when the module is loaded. The information you can provide includes things such as the author, company, copyright date, and a GUID identifier for the module. You can specify requirements for the module, such as the minimum PowerShell version or CLR version required. You also can list the functions, aliases, and variables to be exported from your module.

A benefit of using module manifests is that it is much easier for PowerShell to scan a manifest than to parse a script module file. With PowerShell 3.0, and the recent versions of Windows and Windows Server, the number of delivered modules is very large, and being able to see the contents of a module without parsing hundreds of files is a tremendous time-saver. Manifests also allow you to specify any dependencies for your module, including files that should be executed or loaded when the module is imported.

PowerShell includes a cmdlet called `New-ModuleManifest`, which creates a `.psd1` file for you. Here is the file created by `New-ModuleManifest testmanifest.psd1`:

```
testmanifest.psd1 - Notepad
File  Edit  Format  View  Help
#
# Module manifest for module 'testmanifest'
#
# Generated by: Mike
#
# Generated on: 5/20/2015
#

@{

# Script module or binary module file associated with this manifest.
# RootModule = ''

# Version number of this module.
ModuleVersion = '1.0'

# ID used to uniquely identify this module
GUID = '24832677-5b73-494e-a356-e57cfe19eece'

# Author of this module
Author = 'Mike'

# Company or vendor of this module
CompanyName = 'Unknown'

# Copyright statement for this module
Copyright = '(c) 2015 Mike. All rights reserved.'

# Description of the functionality provided by this module
# Description = ''
```

Listing modules

A module is simply PowerShell's term for a self-contained library or package. PowerShell modules were introduced in Version 2.0. Your operating system is delivered with a number of built-in modules. To see them, you need to use the `Get-Module` cmdlet. If you don't supply any arguments, `Get-Module` outputs a list of all the modules that have been loaded into the current session. To see the list of all the modules that PowerShell can find, you can use the `-ListAvailable` switch.

On my Windows 7 laptop, in a new ISE session, I have only three modules loaded, two "core" modules, and an ISE-specific module, all of which are automatically loaded:

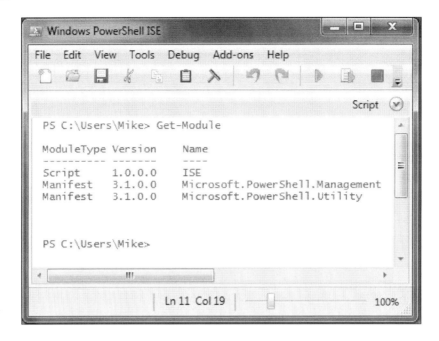

If we use the `-ListAvailable` switch, we can see that there are several modules in several places that I could import into this session:

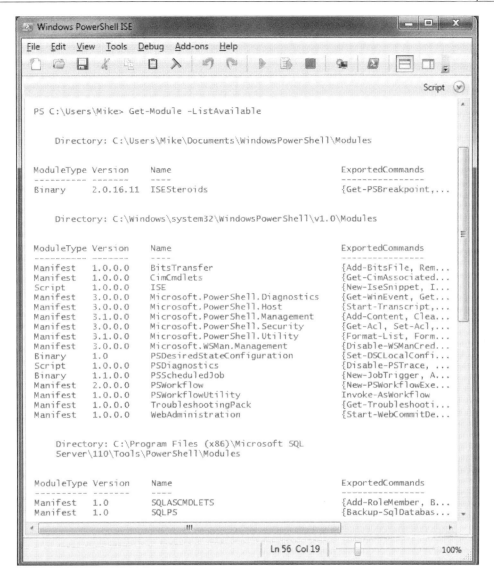

The first column of the output shows the type of the module. In the -ListAvailable output, we can see the Script, Binary, and Manifest modules. Other types of modules that I don't have on my laptop are CIM and Workflow. These types of modules are described in the following table:

Binary, CIM, and Workflow modules are beyond the scope of this book. As a scripter, you will spend most of your time writing scripts and manifest modules.

Summary

In this chapter, we introduced the concept of modules as containers for multiple functions. We showed how to place the modules so that they can be imported easily and how to control the visibility of items contained in a module.

In the next chapter, we will look at how to interact with files in PowerShell.

For Further Reading

- `Get-Help about_Modules`
- `Get-Help Export-ModuleMember`
- `Get-Help about_Requires`

9
File I/O

So far, all the input to commands has been in the form of parameters, and the output has been either to the console (with `write-host`), or to the output stream. In this chapter, we will look at some of the ways that PowerShell gives us to work with files. The topics that will be covered include the following:

- Reading and writing text files
- Working with CSV files
- Output redirection
- Reading and writing objects using CLIXML

Reading and writing text files

One method of reading a text file in PowerShell is to use the `Get-Content` cmdlet. `Get-Content` outputs the contents of the file as a collection of strings. If we have a text file called `Servers.txt` that contains the names of the SQL Servers in our environment, we would use the following code to read the file and get the status of the `MSSQLSERVER` service on the servers. Note that with this code, the file will not contain anything but the server names, each on a separate line with no blank lines:

```
Windows PowerShell ISE
File  Edit  View  Tools  Debug  Add-ons  Help

GetContentExample.ps1  X

1    $servers=get-content servers.txt
2    foreach($server in $servers){
3        get-service -Name MSSQLSERVER -ComputerName $server
4    }

Completed                Ln 3  Col 56                100%
```

If you don't want the file to be split into lines, there is a –Raw switch parameter that causes the cmdlet to output the entire file as a single string. As an example, if we have a text file with three lines, we can see the difference between when we use the default operation and when we use –Raw by counting the number of strings returned:

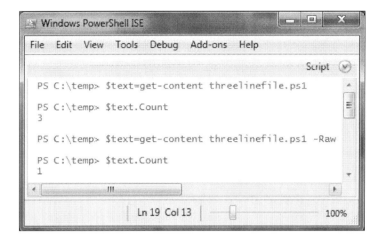

If you want only the beginning or the end of the file, you could use Select-Object with the –First or –Last parameters, but it turns out that Get-Content has this covered as well. To get the beginning of the file, you can use the –TotalCount parameter to specify how many lines to get. To get the end of the file, use the –Tail parameter, instead of the –TotalCount parameter, which lets you specify how many of the end lines to output.

Reminder!

Always filter the pipeline as early as possible. Although, you could achieve the same thing with Select-Object as you can with the –TotalCount and –Tail parameters, filtering at the source (Get-Content) will be faster because less objects will have to be created and passed on to the pipeline.

Writing text files

There are several ways to write to a text file. First, if you have the entire contents of the file in a variable or as the result of a pipeline, you can use the Set-Content cmdlet to write the file as a single unit. For instance, you could read a file with Get-Content, use the .Replace() method to change something, and then write the file back using Set-Content:

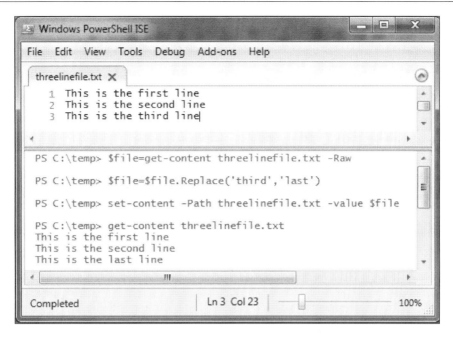

Another useful feature of Set-Content is that you can set the encoding of the file using the -Encoding parameter. The possible values for the encoding are:

- ASCII (the default)
- BigEndianUnicode (UTF-16 big-endian)
- Byte
- String
- Unicode (UTF-16 little-endian)
- UTF7
- UTF8
- Unknown

With all these options, you should have no trouble writing in any format that you need.

Working with CSV files

Comma-separated value files, or CSV files, are a mainstay of the PowerShell world. In the next two sections, we will see how they are very useful, both as input and as output.

Output to CSV for quick reports

If your workplace is anything like mine, you probably work with people who want reports about what is going on. Writing "real" reports in SQL Server reporting services is an option if your data is accessible to SQL server, but they take a while to write and deploy. Obviously, there are reporting packages that you can use as well, such as Crystal Reports, but they can be expensive and take time to write and deploy a report. Most people in IT, though, are fine with Excel as a document format and can work with the data in Excel to create a report.

Outputting objects to CSV files in PowerShell is very simple. The **Export-CSV** cmdlet looks at the properties of the first object in the pipeline and creates a CSV file with a header row containing the names of these properties. It writes the values of these properties in successive lines of the file. Since it uses all the properties of the (first) object, you will probably want to "narrow" down the object using `Select-Object` and the `-Property` parameter to limit the properties that show up in your CSV file.

For example, if you wanted to create a file with the names and lengths of the files in a folder, you could use the following code:

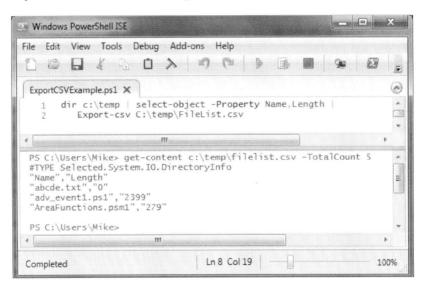

You can see from the output of the `Get-Content` cmdlet that there is a line at the top that indicates the type of objects that were output. You can suppress this line by including the `-NoTypeInformation` switch. You can also see that the column headings and the values are enclosed in quotes and separated by commas. It's possible to change the delimiter to something other than a comma using the `-Delimiter` parameter, but you don't have the option to suppress the quotes.

> **Note**
>
> Although the cmdlets refer to CSV, using a delimiter such as `` `t `` (a tab) would obviously create a tab-separated value file or a TSV. For some kinds of data, TSV might be a preferred format, and programs like Excel are able to load TSV files just fine.

The Invoke-Item cmdlet

You can easily open a CSV file in Excel (or whatever application is associated with CSV files on your system) using the `Invoke-Item` cmdlet. `Invoke-Item` performs the default action associated with a particular file. You can think of it as double-clicking on an item in the File Explorer. If you have Excel, the default action for CSV files is to open them in Excel. To easily open the output file we created in the last section, we would use `Invoke-Item c:\temp\filelist.csv`, and it would pop up looking like a spreadsheet as follows:

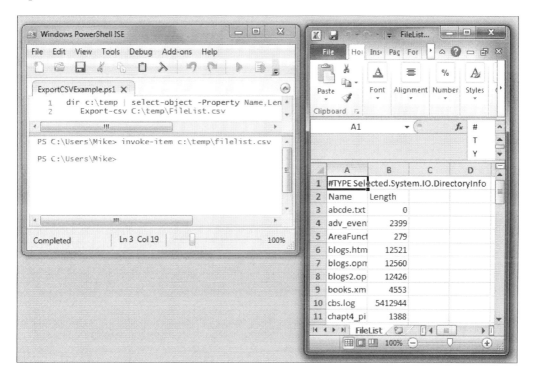

At this point, it can be manipulated just like a normal spreadsheet, so it's easy for people who haven't learned PowerShell yet to work with it.

Import from CSV for quick objects

Since PowerShell cmdlets work on objects, it's convenient to be able to read a file as a sequence of objects rather than as strings, like you would from Get-Content. Just as Export-CSV takes objects and writes them to a file, Import-CSV reads a CSV file and outputs objects with the properties that are named in the header.

An easy example to understand would be a CSV file that contains a server list with the name of each server, as well as the type of the server (Web, Database, or File), and whom to contact, if there are problems with each server:

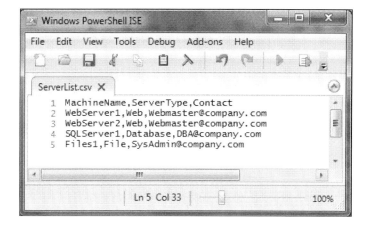

With this CSV file, we can easily read this into a variable using Import-CSV. As Import-CSV creates objects, we can refer to the rows of this CSV file using properties. Getting a summary of our servers using the Group-Object cmdlet is a simple matter:

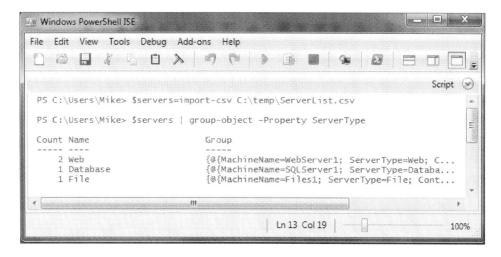

PowerShell streams and redirection

We've talked about the output stream, but it turns out that PowerShell has quite a few streams besides this. Here's the list, including one that was introduced in PowerShell 5:

Stream	Number	Contents
Output	1	Output from commands
Error	2	Error messages
Warning	3	Warning messages
Debug	4	Debug messages
Verbose	5	Verbose output
Information	6	General information (PowerShell 5)

Similar to DOS, you can redirect streams to a file using the greater-than symbol (>). For example, you can send a directory listing to a file as follows:

```
Dir c:\temp >c:\temp\files.txt
```

The output is formatted according to standard PowerShell formatting, but since it's just a text file, you can't recreate the objects that you started with. Also, unlike with Set-Content, you can't control the output encoding, which is always Unicode if you use the redirection operator.

Other types of redirection operators

In addition to the single greater-than symbol, there are a number of other redirection operators that append (using two greater-than symbols) and combine streams (such as 2>&1, which merges the error stream to the output stream using the numbers found in the table). As there a number of streams and a variety of operators, you should refer to the about_redirection help topic for a complete description.

The out-file cmdlet

A final way to redirect output is to use the out-file cmdlet. Unlike the redirect operator, out-file includes an –Encoding parameter that lets you change the encoding. The values for this parameter are the same as the Set-Content cmdlet. The main difference between Set-Content and Out-File is that Out-File accepts pipeline input. So, you will use Out-File as the last command in a pipeline to send the output to a file.

For instance, the redirection we performed with the redirection operator would be expressed using `Out-File` as follows:

```
Dir c:\temp | out-file C:\temp\files.txt
```

I don't know about you, but this is a lot easier for me to read. If you want to append to an existing file, the `-Append` switch is what you're looking for. You don't get to combine streams as you can with the redirection operators, but for general purpose output redirection, `Out-File` is a good candidate.

CLIXML – a special type of XML

You've seen how we can use `Export-CSV` to write objects to a file and that we can read these objects back using `Import-CSV`. One limitation of using the CSV format is that it is a flat format, meaning that you get a list of properties that have simple values. If you need to output arbitrary objects to a file and need to store more interesting values than strings, you should probably look at the CLIXML cmdlets, `Export-CLIXML` and `Import-CLIXML`. CLIXML is an XML-based format to serialize objects.

When you export objects using `Export-CLIXML`, it looks at the list of properties that may be value properties (such as `string` or `int` values) or they may be objects themselves. If they are objects, `Export-CLIXML` will look at the properties of the properties. It will continue this process until it reaches a predetermined depth. The default value of depth is "2", but you can override this using the `-Depth` parameter.

To see how this works, let's get a particular service and export it to a file using this command:

```
get-service MSSQLSERVER | Export-CLIXML -path C:\temp\SQL.clixml
```

Looking at the following output, you can see that it's XML, but it's still fairly readable. The file includes the list of type names (the type of the object as well as any ancestor types), followed by a list of properties. Some of them start with an `S` or a `B`, denoting String or Boolean, and others start with OBJ or NIL meaning objects that are either populated or empty:

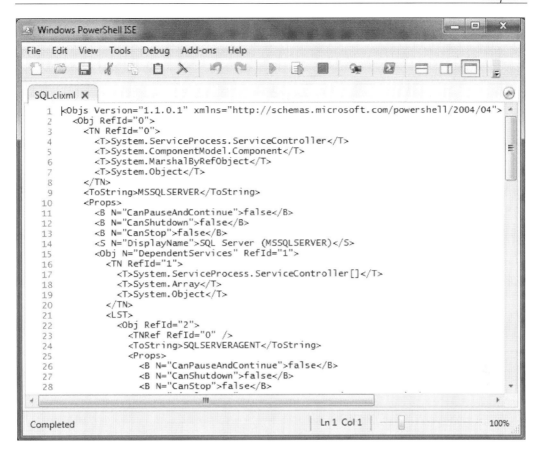

Reading a CLIXML file with `Import-CLIXML` builds a complex object, but it's not quite the same object that you started with for three reasons, as follows:

- The object was only written to a limited depth, so we could have lost some details

- The methods are not included in the recreated object, only the properties

- Since we didn't use the constructor for the type of object we need, the type of the object is now slightly different

We can see the differences using `get-member` on the imported object:

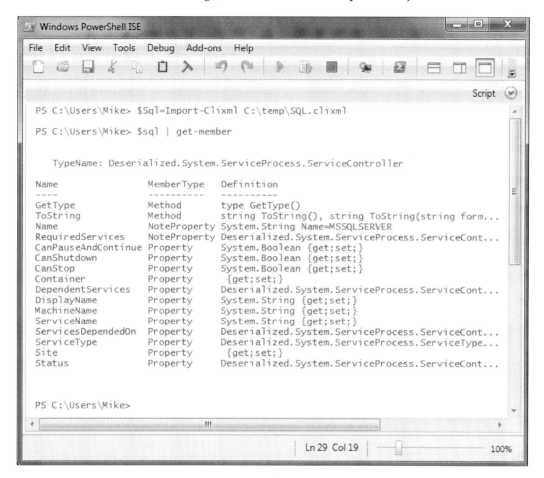

You try it!

Use the `Get-Member` cmdlet along with the `Get-Service` cmdlet to see what members are present in an actual `ServiceController` object. Then, compare this with the previous screenshot to see that the `Deserialized` object is actually different.

Note that the type of the object now starts with **Deserialized**. This is because the process of writing an object is called serialization, and the process of recreating an object from a serialized format is called deserialization. You might, also, hear such objects being referred to as "rehydrated" or "unwired". The point is that this object, for instance, is no longer connected to the MSSQLSERVER service on my laptop like the original object was.

Summary

PowerShell has a very rich set of cmdlets that deal with file input and output. We've seen how to read and write text files, CSV files, and CLIXML files. We, also, looked at how to use redirection to cause PowerShell to write streams to files or combine streams together.

In the next chapter, we will look at one way by which PowerShell can communicate with different kinds of software and components on a computer, using WMI and CIM. These capabilities greatly expand PowerShell's power, and causes it to be an almost universal tool in the Microsoft environment.

For further reading

- Get-Help Get-Content
- Get-Help Set-Content
- Get-Help Out-File
- Get-Help about_Redirection
- Get-Help Export-CSV
- Get-Help Import-CSV
- Get-Help Export-CLIXML
- Get-Help Import-CLIXML

10
WMI and CIM

We've looked at several kinds of cmdlets so far in this book, but until now, each cmdlet has been working with a specific kind of object. In this chapter, we will look at the WMI and CIM cmdlets, which will allow us to look at a seemingly unlimited range of object types. In this chapter, we will cover the following topics:

- What are WMI and CIM?
- A WMI/CIM glossary
- Retrieving objects via WMI and CIM
- Calling methods via WMI and CIM
- The CDXML modules

What is WMI?

Getting objects from cmdlets is what PowerShell is all about. Unfortunately, there are more kinds of objects that we might be interested in than PowerShell has cmdlets for. This was definitely the case during the time of PowerShell 1.0, which only had less than a hundred cmdlets. What do we do about the objects for which PowerShell doesn't have an explicit cmdlet? The answer involves **Windows Management Instrumentation (WMI)**. WMI was introduced as a common interface to manage operating system objects all the way back in Windows NT. WMI provides a uniform way to retrieve objects, which allows us to inspect and even change the state of components, processes, and other objects. Before we look at specific WMI information, it's important to understand how objects are stored in WMI.

WMI organization

The WMI objects are stored in a repository that is local to a computer system. The repository is divided into several namespaces, each of which provides different objects. Inside a namespace there are the WMI classes, each of which describes a certain type of object. Finally, there are the WMI instances, which are specific examples of a WMI class.

An analogy would help to make more sense of this. If we think of the WMI repository like a filing cabinet, the comparison might go something as follows:

- The repository is a filing cabinet
- A namespace is a drawer in the cabinet
- A class is a folder in the drawer
- An instance is a piece of paper in the drawer

The information that you want is found on the piece of paper, that is, in the WMI instance.

Finding WMI classes

The first thing to know about the WMI classes is that there are a ton of them. So many, in fact, that you will almost certainly never need to use most of them. As there are so many classes, finding the class that you want to work with can be interesting. The `Get-WMIObject` cmdlet has a parameter called `-List`, which lets you get a list of the classes installed on your computer. Combining this cmdlet with `Measure-Object` shows that my computer (Windows 7) has over a thousand classes in the default namespace:

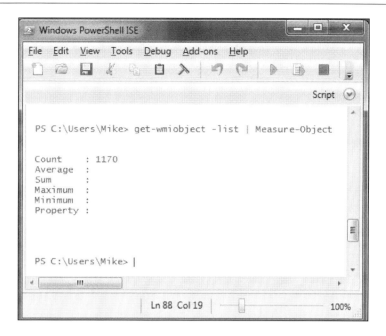

You clearly don't want to look through a list of so many items, so you can narrow down the list with the -Class parameter, which accepts wildcards. For instance, to find classes that deal with the processor, you might do this:

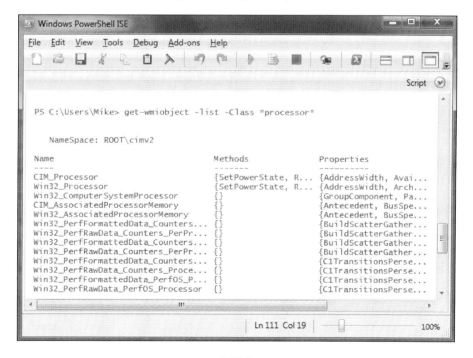

The first two in the list (CIM_Processor and Win32_Processor) are the results that are most useful in this case. Depending on what wildcard you use, you may need to look at several classes to find the one that is most appropriate.

> **Note**
> The classes beginning with Win32 are based on the classes beginning with CIM. Generally, I stick with the Win32 classes, but they usually have almost the same information.

Retrieving objects with Get-WMIObject

If you know the name of a class and what namespace that class belongs to, it is simple to retrieve the class using the Get-WMIObject cmdlet. For instance, there is a class that describes the installed operating system called Win32_OperatingSystem contained in the default (root\CIMV2) namespace. To retrieve this class, either of these command-lines will work:

```
Get-WMIObject -class Win32_OperatingSystem
Get-WMIObject -class Win32_OperatingSystem -namespace root\CIMV2
```

The output here is formatted, so you will probably want to use Select-Object -property * to see all the properties. In this case, there are 73 properties, which are too many for a screenshot.

You try it!

Use `Get-WMIObject` with the `Win32_OperatingSystem` class and
look through the properties. You might make a note of the properties
that you think would be useful. As you use WMI (and CIM) more and
more, you will find a number of classes and properties that you will
come back to over and over again. Hence, having a list of "favorites"
can be a real life-saver.

One thing you probably noticed with `Win32_OperatingSystem` is that only one
object (instance) was retrieved by the cmdlet. This makes sense, because there's
only one operating system running on a computer at a time (not counting VMs,
of course). The other classes might return zero, one, or any number of instances.

A class that should be easy to understand is the `Win32_Service` class. This class
represents the Windows services that are installed in your operating system.
You can see the beginning of the formatted output in the following screenshot:

You might ask why we would use WMI to get information about services when we have a perfectly good cmdlet (Get-Service) that is designed to do this. Even though we can see only a few properties of each WMI service object in the preceding output, theres enough information to illustrate an important point. The first object in the output, AdobeARMService, shows six properties. Comparing these properties with the full output of the Get-Service cmdlet reveals that the Name and State properties of the WMI object have analogous properties (Name and Status) in the Get-Service object, but the other four properties (including ProcessID) are missing from Get-Service:

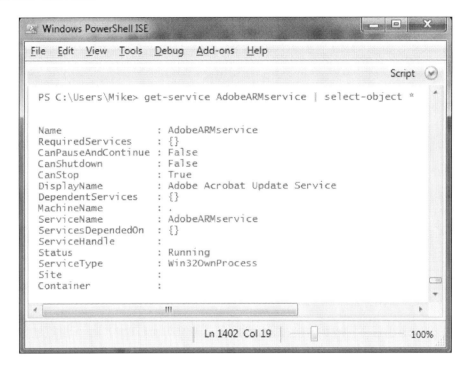

Remember that WMI is a very mature technology that has been in use for over 20 years. As WMI is so well established, most aspects of the Windows ecosystem is covered very well by WMI.

Tip!

In addition to keeping track of the interesting WMI classes, you might also want to make a note of the properties of WMI instances that are missing from the objects output by other PowerShell cmdlets. Often, WMI provides the easiest way to get some information.

Getting the right instance

With `Win32_ComputerSystem`, we didn't have to worry about which instance was returned because there was only one. The next class we looked at was `Win32_Service`, which returned multiple objects, one for each service on the computer. In order to select specific instances, we can use the `-Filter` parameter.

Since WMI covers thousands of different kinds of classes, it would be impossible for `Get-WMIObject` to have specific parameters to help us narrow down which objects we would like to see. For instance, if we use `Get-Service` to look at services, we can use the `-Name` parameter to filter by name. Not all WMI objects have a name property, so it wouldn't make sense to have a parameter to filter by this single property. The solution is to have a query language called **WMI Query Language (WQL)**, similar to SQL, and a single parameter called `-Filter` that takes the WHERE clause of the WQL query in order to filter the objects.

WQL syntax

WQL syntax is very simple to use, and is very similar to SQL. In the WQL filter, you can use the property names of classes, constants, and operators to build the conditions you are looking for. For example, to return only the `AdobeARMService` instance from the `Win32_Service` class, you could use a filter of `"Name='AdobeARMService'"`. Note that I have used double quotes around the filter and single quotes around the string value of the `Name` property. The full `Get-WMIObject` statement and output looks as follows:

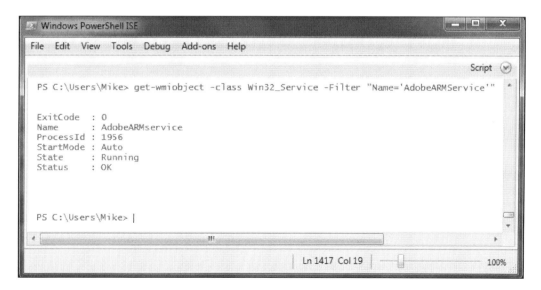

Filters can be more complex as well. Consider the `Win32_LogicalDisk` class, which contains an instance for each drive on the local computer:

If we wanted to list all the drives that had less than 10GB free and didn't care about the removable, we could use a filter as follows:

```
-Filter "DriveType=3 and FreeSpace< 10737418240"
```

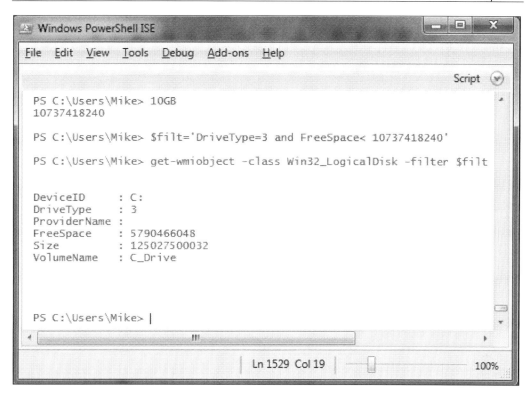

Here, you can see that I have calculated the value of 10GB because WQL doesn't understand units, and also, I have used a variable to hold the filter in order to keep the line shorter.

Note!

Although WQL filters look like SQL syntax, there are crucial differences. You can use comparison operators (=, < >, >, <. <=, >=, LIKE) in the expressions and can link multiple expressions together with AND and OR. You can also group expressions using parentheses. Another important thing to remember is that the WQL strings use backslash as the escape character. For more details, including how to use the WQL queries, refer to the About_WQL help topic.

Calling methods

When dealing with WMI, there are two kinds of methods that come into play, instance methods and class methods. Calling the WMI instance methods is similar to calling methods on any PowerShell object, that is, using dot-notation. For instance, WMI objects from the `Win32_Service` class have a `StartService()` method defined in them, which we can verify using `Get-Member`:

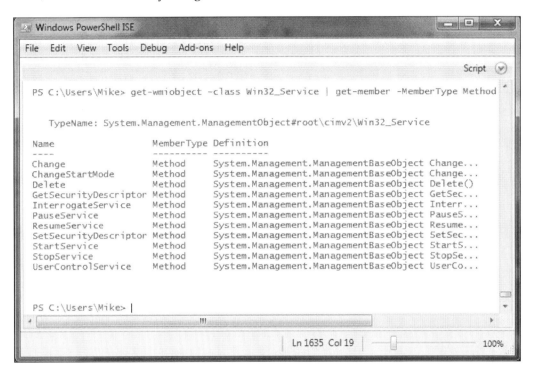

To call this method, we can store the instance in a variable and use the variable to call the method. Note that the method outputs a structured result type. The `ReturnValue` property of the output gives us the outcome of the operation. A value of zero means success. An example of a successful method invocation can be seen in the following screenshot:

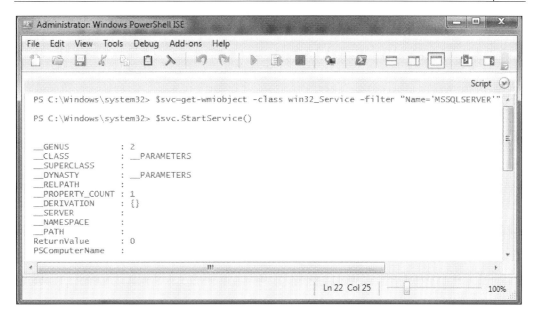

Note

You might notice that the preceding screenshot is an elevated session. If you try to start a service in a non-elevated session, you get a `ReturnValue` of 2, which means "warning".

WMI and CIM

PowerShell 3.0 introduced the **Common Information Model (CIM)** cmdlets to access WMI repositories. The WMI cmdlets are still present, but they have been superseded by the CIM cmdlets that can perform all the same functions. From a functional level, the CIM cmdlets are similar to the WMI cmdlets. The main difference is the communication that the cmdlets perform with the target computer. The WMI cmdlets use the DCOM protocol, which is a pretty standard thing to do on Windows systems, especially 20 years ago when WMI was created. Unfortunately, DCOM is kind of a mess from a firewall standpoint, as it uses a range of ports (over 16000 ports by default) that need to be open in order to function. In a data center situation, requiring this many ports to be opened in the firewalls is something that network engineers frown upon.

The CIM cmdlets, by default, use **Web Services for Management (WS-MAN)**, the protocol that PowerShell remoting is based on. WS-MAN uses a single port, and has a number of other properties that make it ideal from a networking standpoint. Finally, the CIM cmdlets support sessions, which allow you to reuse a connection to a computer or a set of computers for multiple requests, which can dramatically reduce the network traffic for some workloads.

If you're just looking at the WMI repositories on the local box like we've done in the examples of this chapter, both sets of cmdlets will work fine. If you're looking at the WMI classes across multiple computers in a network, you will need to consider firewall rules and whether WS-MAN is enabled. These are beyond the scope of this book, but are good to make a note of.

The CIM cmdlets

The two main CIM cmdlets that you will use are `Get-CIMClass` and `Get-CIMInstance`. Although `Get-WMIObject` is used to retrieve both the WMI classes (with `-List`) and WMI instances (without `-List`), these roles are carried out by separate CIM cmdlets. Using `Get-CIMClass` is virtually identical to using `Get-WMIObject` with the `-List` switch. We can recreate the processor example from earlier in the chapter with `Get-CIMClass` as follows:

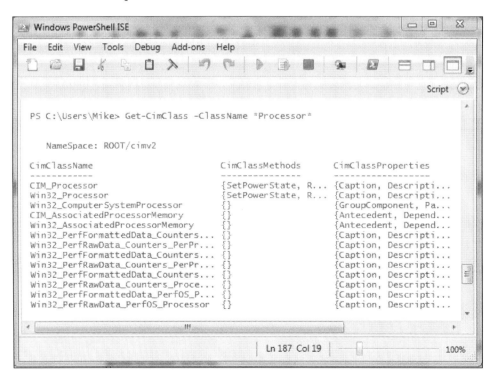

Retrieving instances is done, of course, with `Get-CIMInstance`. Filters work exactly like they do with `Get-WMIObject`. Also, the objects output by these two cmdlets are the same, so working with the results will be exactly the same.

CDXML modules

One of the drawbacks of using the WMI or CIM cmdlets is that you don't get to use parameters that are specific to the properties of the WMI class you are dealing with. For instance, when we looked at the `Win32_LogicalDisk` instances, it would have been really nice to have parameters such as `DriveType` or `Name` to easily filter the output without having to use a WQL filter statement. In PowerShell 3.0, the concept of a CDXML module was introduced. CDXML modules allow you to create an XML description of the cmdlets and the associated parameters dealing with a WMI class, and the PowerShell engine creates the cmdlets for you when you import the module.

The CDXML modules have two main advantages, as follows:

- The module is XML, so no coding is necessary.
- End users get to use parameters that are specific to the type of object rather than a generic `-Filter` parameter

In PowerShell 4.0, the majority of modules on a server will be CDXML modules, because they are easy to write.

Summary

In this chapter, we have taken a quick look at the basics of using the WMI and CIM cmdlets. It should be clear that there is a lot of information in the WMI repository, and these cmdlets are essential tools for PowerShell scripters. With the introduction of CDXML modules, we're also seeing more cmdlets that are customized to specific WMI classes, making their usage even easier.

In the final chapter, we will look at administering Internet Information Services (IIS).

For further reading

- `Get-Help about_WMI`

- `Get-Help about_WMI_Cmdlets`

- `Get-Help about_WQL`

- WMI Result codes:
  `https://msdn.microsoft.com/en-us/library/aa394574(v=vs.85).aspx`

- Get-Help about_CIMSession

- Article summarizing CIM/WMI/OMI/DMTF terminology:
  `http://powershell.org/wp/2015/04/24/management-information-the-omicimwmimidmtf-dictionary/`

11
Web Server Administration

In this chapter, we will learn how to deal with **Internet Information Services** (**IIS**), the web server that ships with Windows servers. We will specifically look at the following topics:

- Installing IIS
- The WebAdministration module
- Starting, stopping, and restarting IIS
- Creating virtual directories and web applications
- Working with app pools

Installing IIS

Before we install IIS, we need to determine whether it is already installed. This is done differently in a client OS, such as Windows 8.1, rather than in a server OS such as Server 2012R2.

Detecting and installing IIS in Windows 8.1

In a client OS, the cmdlet to use is `Get-WindowsOptionalFeature`, and the name of the feature to look for is `IIS-WebServerRole`. The `-Online` switch tells the cmdlet to examine the OS running on the computer rather than looking in a Windows image. In the following screenshot, you can see that IIS is not enabled on my Windows 8.1 computer:

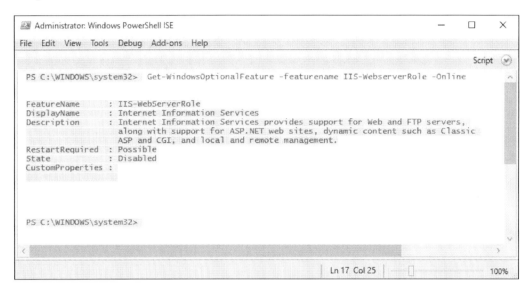

To install IIS, you can use the `Enable-WindowsOptionalFeature` cmdlet using the `IIS-WebServerRole` feature name again and the `-Online` switch. I also added the `-All` switch to tell `Enable-WindowsOptionalFeature` to enable any required features as well:

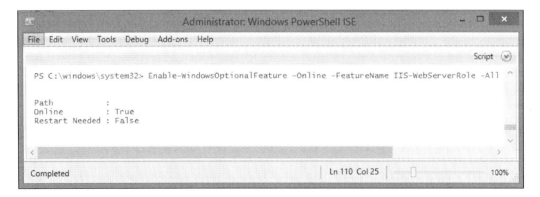

Detecting and installing IIS in Server 2012R2

The process to detect and install IIS in Server 2012R2 is similar to what we did in Windows 8.1, but it uses slightly different cmdlets. To find out whether IIS is enabled, we will use the `Get-WindowsFeature` cmdlet and we will specify `Web-*` as the name of the feature we're looking for:

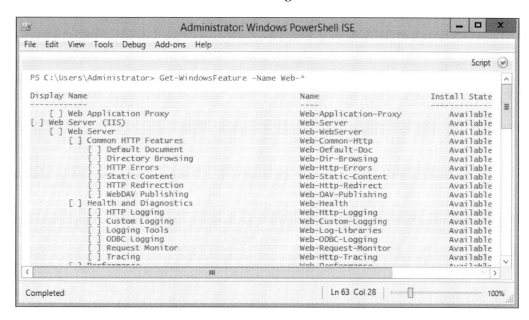

This output is organized very nicely, mimicking the Windows Feature control panel applet. You can easily see the hierarchy of features, and the state of the feature is shown in the box to the left of the display name. In our case, we want to install the `Web-Server` feature. We can do this using the `Add-WindowsFeature` cmdlet:

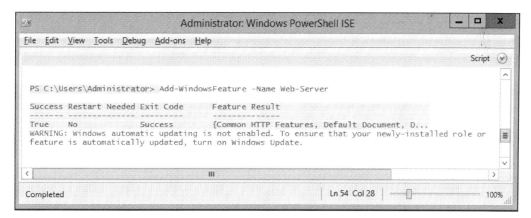

Verifying IIS

For either a client or server OS, we would verify that IIS is enabled using the associated Get- cmdlet, but it makes more sense to me to try to load a web page. IIS configures a default web site with a standard web page, so we should be able to navigate to http://localhost and know immediately whether everything is working well:

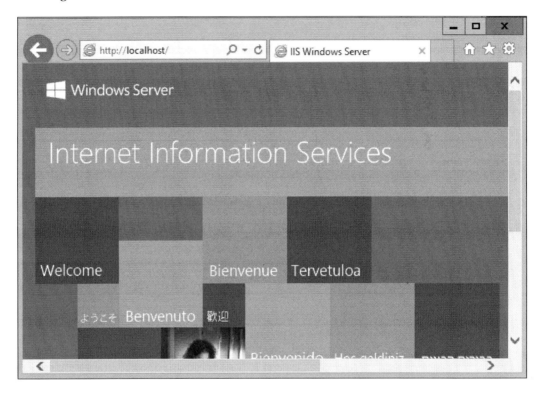

The WebAdministration module

Once IIS is installed, we need to import the WebAdministration module to interact with IIS (using Import-Module WebAdministration). Using the Get-Command cmdlet to find the Get- cmdlets in the module is a good way to get an idea about what the module allows us to work with:

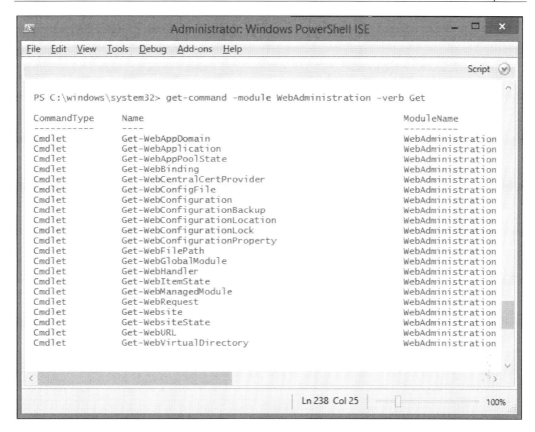

Here, we can see that we have cmdlets to deal with sites, virtual directories, applications, bindings, configuration, and much more. Another thing that is worth mentioning at this point is that the WebAdministration module also adds a new PSProvider called WebAdministration and a PSDrive called IIS, which exposes a hierarchical view of the IIS installation. Remember that PSDrives are how PowerShell exposes hierarchical data. In this case, the IIS configuration is treated in a similar way to a drive.

You try it!

Starting with CD IIS:, explore the IIS installation using the DIR (Get-ChildItem) cmdlet. Don't forget to change back to a filesystem drive when you're done.

Starting, stopping, and restarting IIS

Since you can run command-line programs in PowerShell, the IISReset command can be used to start, stop, and restart IIS using the /START, /STOP, and /RESTART switches:

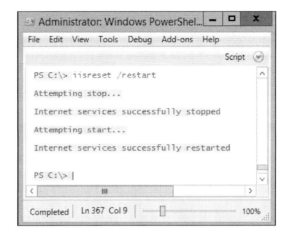

If you want to start or stop a particular website rather than the entire IIS installation, you need to use the Start-WebSite and Stop-WebSite cmdlets. They both have a –Name parameter that allows you to specify which site you want to work with. In the following screenshot, I am stopping and starting a website called Test. Also, I have used the Get-WebSite cmdlet after each step to show that the Test site stopped and started correctly:

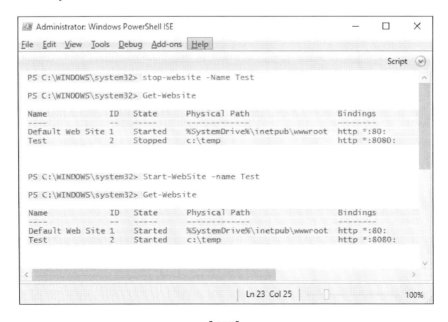

Creating virtual directories and web applications

Virtual directories and web applications are the different options to contain content in IIS. A virtual directory is a pointer to a location on the disk where the content actually resides. A web application, in the IIS terminology, is a virtual directory that also has the ability to run in a different worker process than its parent.

To create a virtual directory, we will use the New-WebVirtualDirectory cmdlet and supply the -Name and -PhysicalPath parameters. Also, we will need to specify the site and we can do this in one of the following two ways:

1. Use Set-Location (CD) in the IIS drive and navigate to the desired site.
2. Specify the site on the command line.

In the following screenshot, we will illustrate the first method:

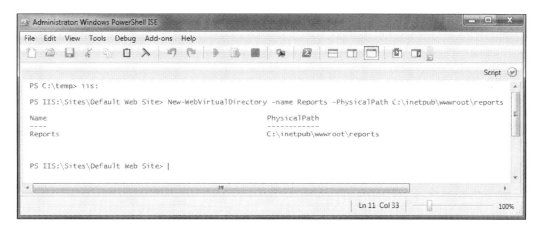

If you are working with a website besides the default site (Default Web Site), you will need to set the location to this site. For instance, to create a virtual directory in the Test site, you would use Set-Location IIS:\Sites\Test\.

The process to create a web application is similar. The New-WebApplication cmdlet takes –Name and –PhysicalPath parameters as well as a –Site parameter that can be supplied in the same fashion as with New-WebVirtualDirectory. Here, we create a new web application called ReportsApp in the root of the default web site. Note that the cmdlet expects the physical path to be an existing directory, or you can use the –Force switch to make the cmdlet create the folder for you. I've tried to create a web application with a path that doesn't exist, as shown in the following screenshot. After receiving an error, I retried with –Force and was successful.

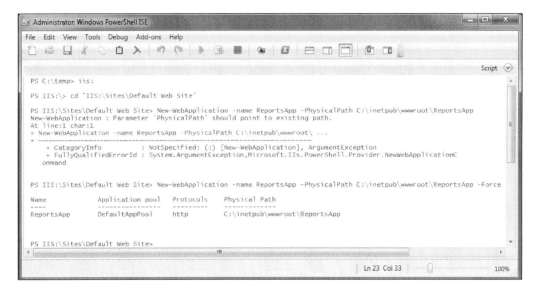

If we wanted the new application to run in a specific application pool, we would have used the –ApplicationPool parameter to specify its name.

You can easily see the virtual directories and web applications with the IIS drive. After using CD (Set-Location) in the \Sites\Default Web Site folder, DIR (Get-ChildItem) shows all of the folders, files, virtual directories, and web applications:

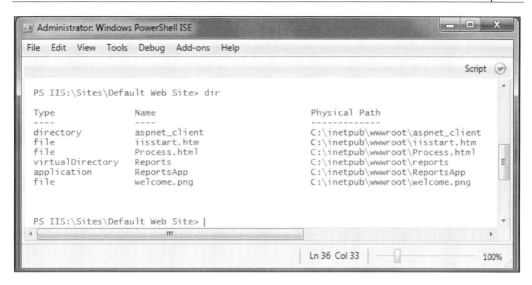

Working with application pools

Given the fantastic cmdlet support for virtual directories and web applications, I was surprised to find that there isn't a `Get-WebAppPool` cmdlet. There is a `Get-WebAppPoolState` cmdlet, but the formatted output isn't particularly useful.

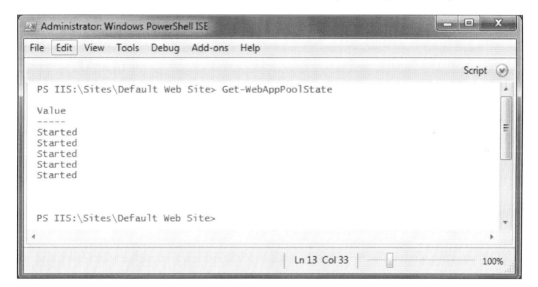

From the previous screenshot, you can see that there are five application pools and they have all been started, but you don't know what they are called. If one showed **Stopped**, for instance, you wouldn't know which one you needed to start. Adding `Select-Object -Property *` helps sometimes, but the values aren't easy to use.

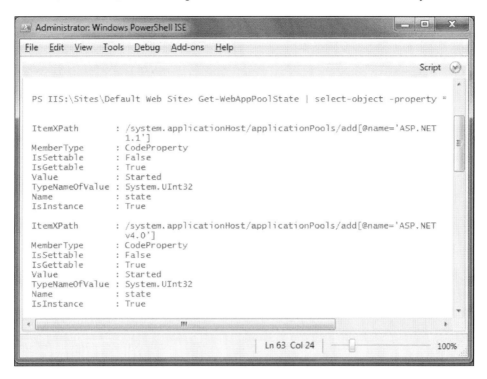

Since the name of the application pool is embedded in an `XPath` expression, it is not very easy to work with. Fortunately for us, the application pools are easy to find in the IIS drive, so we can craft our own function to return the app pools.

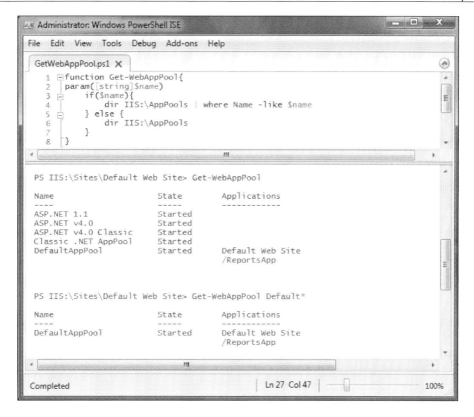

Creating application pools

We can create an app pool using the New-WebAppPool cmdlet, which only has one interesting parameter called -Name. We're going to create an app pool called ReportPool and later configure the ReportApp web application to run in this app pool:

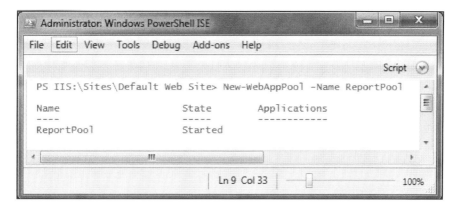

Switching an application to run in this pool involves a PSProvider-related cmdlet called Set-ItemProperty:

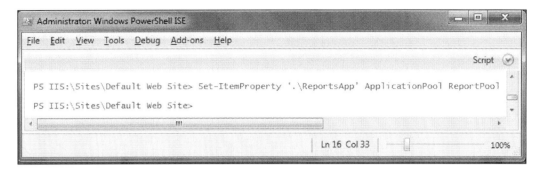

We can easily verify that the changes worked using our Get-WebAppPool function from earlier in the chapter:

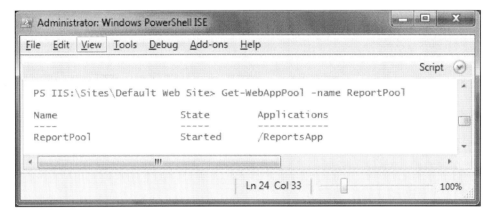

Summary

In this chapter, we saw how to work with IIS, including the installation and validation. We created virtual directories, web applications, and application pools, and learned how to use the IIS drive.

For further reading

- Get-Help Get-WindowsOptionalFeature

- Get-Help Enable-WindowsOptionalFeature

- Get-Help Get-WindowsFeature

- Get-Help Add-WindowsFeature

- The WebAdministration module:
  https://technet.microsoft.com/en-us/library/ee790599.aspx

- Get-help Start-Website

- Get-help Stop-Website

- Get-help Get-Website

- Get-help New-WebVirtualDirectory

- Get-help New-WebApplication

- Get-help Get-WebAppPoolState

- Get-help New-WebAppPool

- Get-help Set-ItemProperty

Next Steps

The goal of this book has been to get you started with PowerShell. To this end, we have looked at several broad topics, such as:

- Navigating PowerShell with `Get-Command`, `Get-Help`, and `Get-Member`
- Using the Pipeline to combine the commands
- Packaging code in scripts, functions, and modules
- Interacting with files and WMI
- Administering IIS

These skills will take you far in PowerShell, but this is just the beginning of what you can do. Here, I have collected some suggested "next steps" that you will find useful as skills to add to your PowerShell repertoire:

- Explore advanced functions, such as:
    - Using common parameters
    - Pipeline the input
    - Parameter validation

- PowerShell Remoting
- PowerShell Workflows
- Desired State Configuration
- Explore miscellaneous PowerShell topics, including the following:
    - Working with .NET and COM objects
    - Working with SQL Server data
    - Building a GUI

- Administering Microsoft systems such as:

  ° Exchange
  ° SQL Server
  ° System Center

You should have no trouble finding resources to guide you through any of these topics. If you are stuck, the PowerShell community on StackOverflow, PowerShell. org (`http://powershell.org/wp/`), and reddit are very strong and encouraging to scripters at all levels of expertise.

Index

W

Thank you for buying
Getting Started with PowerShell

About Packt Publishing

Packt, pronounced 'packed', published its first book, *Mastering phpMyAdmin for Effective MySQL Management*, in April 2004, and subsequently continued to specialize in publishing highly focused books on specific technologies and solutions.

Our books and publications share the experiences of your fellow IT professionals in adapting and customizing today's systems, applications, and frameworks. Our solution-based books give you the knowledge and power to customize the software and technologies you're using to get the job done. Packt books are more specific and less general than the IT books you have seen in the past. Our unique business model allows us to bring you more focused information, giving you more of what you need to know, and less of what you don't.

Packt is a modern yet unique publishing company that focuses on producing quality, cutting-edge books for communities of developers, administrators, and newbies alike. For more information, please visit our website at www.packtpub.com.

About Packt Open Source

In 2010, Packt launched two new brands, Packt Open Source and Packt Enterprise, in order to continue its focus on specialization. This book is part of the Packt Open Source brand, home to books published on software built around open source licenses, and offering information to anybody from advanced developers to budding web designers. The Open Source brand also runs Packt's Open Source Royalty Scheme, by which Packt gives a royalty to each open source project about whose software a book is sold.

Writing for Packt

We welcome all inquiries from people who are interested in authoring. Book proposals should be sent to author@packtpub.com. If your book idea is still at an early stage and you would like to discuss it first before writing a formal book proposal, then please contact us; one of our commissioning editors will get in touch with you.

We're not just looking for published authors; if you have strong technical skills but no writing experience, our experienced editors can help you develop a writing career, or simply get some additional reward for your expertise.

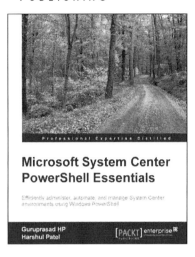

Microsoft System Center PowerShell Essentials

ISBN: 978-1-78439-714-2   Paperback: 140 pages

Efficiently administer, automate, and manage System Center environments using Windows PowerShell

1. Create powerful automation scripts for System Center products using PowerShell.

2. Discover PowerShell techniques to efficiently handle SCCM, SCOM, and SCSM with real-time examples and sample codes.

3. A step-by-step guide with practical examples and best practices that teaches you to effectively use PowerShell in System Center environment.

Mastering Windows PowerShell Scripting

ISBN: 978-1-78217-355-7   Paperback: 282 pages

Master the art of automating and managing your Windows environment using PowerShell

1. Construct scripts by following proven best practices to automate redundant tasks.

2. Delve into real-world examples to understand how to simplify the management of your Windows environment.

3. Get to grips with PowerShell's advanced functions and effectively administer your system.

Please check **www.PacktPub.com** for information on our titles

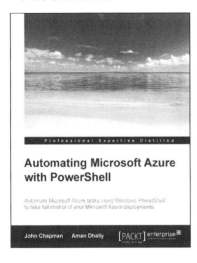

Automating Microsoft Azure
Automate Microsoft Azure tasks using Windows PowerShell
to take full control of your Microsoft Azure deployments

John Chapman   Aman Dhally

Automating Microsoft Azure with PowerShell

ISBN: 978-1-78439-887-3   Paperback: 156 pages

Automate Microsoft Azure tasks using Windows
PowerShell to take full control of your Microsoft
Azure deployments

1. Deploy and manage virtual machines,
   virtual networks, and an online database for
   application provisioning, maintenance, and
   high availability of your data.

2. Upload your movies, data, and disk images
   to the cloud with just a single line of
   PowerShell code.

3. A pragmatic guide full of hands-on
   examples on managing Microsoft Azure
   using PowerShell.

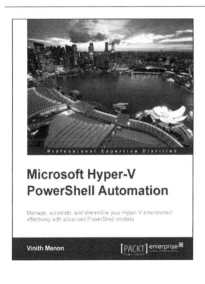

Microsoft Hyper-V
PowerShell Automation
Manage, automate, and streamline your Hyper-V environment
effectively with advanced PowerShell cmdlets

Vinith Menon

Microsoft Hyper-V PowerShell Automation

ISBN: 978-1-78439-153-9   Paperback: 124 pages

Manage, automate, and streamline your
Hyper-V environment effectively with advanced
PowerShell cmdlets

1. Explore the new features in Hyper-V in
   Windows Server 2012 R2 and also learn to
   automate them using PowerShell.

2. Take advantage of numerous Hyper-V best
   practices for administrators with re-usable
   PowerShell scripts.

3. Implement your learning immediately with
   practical instructions and examples.

Please check **www.PacktPub.com** for information on our titles